IN THE IMAGE OF CHRIST

For to me
    to live
        is Christ . . .
St. Paul: Philippians 1:21

Let us rejoice
    and give thanks.
    Not only have we become
    Christians,
but we have become Christ!
St. Augustine: In Joan., 21

Our Saviour shares prerogatives
peculiarly His own with the Church
    in such a way that she may portray,
    in her whole life,
        both exterior and interior,
a most faithful image of Christ.
Pius XII: *Mystici Corporis Christi*

In the
IMAGE OF CHRIST

JOHN L. MURPHY

THE BRUCE PUBLISHING COMPANY
MILWAUKEE

Nihil obstat: JOHN A. SCHULIEN, S.T.D., *Censor librorum*
Imprimatur: ✠ ROMANUS R. ATKIELSKI, D.D., *Vicarius Generalis* et
 Episcopus Auxiliaris
Milwauchiae, Die 1, Mensis iulii, 1954

Library of Congress Catalog Card Number: 54-9868

COPYRIGHT, 1954, THE BRUCE PUBLISHING COMPANY
MADE IN THE UNITED STATES OF AMERICA

To
KATE AND JIM

Acknowledgment is gratefully made to
Fides Publishers Association, Chicago,
for permission to quote from the writings
of Cardinal Suhard as contained in their
collection, *The Church Today* (1953).

PREFACE

THE chapters of this book might be described as a "Set of Variations Upon a Theme by St. Paul." Each chapter will say the same thing basically: the Christian is called to be "another Christ," and because of that he must *be* Christ in all that he does. He must make his own the interests and the concerns of Christ; he must do all within his power to bring Christ and His ideals to the world about him.

In one way, it might be enough to state the theme, and go no further. The men and women in every walk of life might figure out just how that fact of Christian faith fits into their own particular life. It might help, however, to have the application laid out beforehand, to serve as a guide on the way. Certainly what I have written is not an exhaustive treatment of any profession. It is intended to be a book of suggestions, and nothing more. I have tried to indicate a rather broad outline of life in Christ and the Church. Writing in such a broad outline, I have not attempted to settle any difficult problems either. It has been written with the hope of stimulating a certain interest on the part of each reader for this general mission of the Church, and its particular application to his own life.

In stressing the obligation of the doctor or the worker or the priest or the television star to cultivate a certain outlook, I wouldn't want it to appear that I was speaking only to them. They have their special tasks, but the demands of modern life require us all to think about many different problems. This is particularly true in our American way of life where so much is left up to the current of popular opinion, and, in some cases, to the popular vote. A disinterested public can effectively tie the hands of the most zealous apostle in such a circumstance.

What follows, then, might help every reader to gain a bit more of an insight into the role of the Church in the modern world. Understanding that role is a part of understanding our faith. There are many men today who would like to restrict the religious life of the individual to his private life; men who would like to keep the Church in the sacristy. But that is not Christianity. Christianity is a *commitment* to the world, not an escape from it, nor a denial of it. It is intended to be lived *in* the world. As Abbé Hasseveldt remarks: "Jesus did not say: 'I intend to establish a Church where you will be sheltered, where you will have your own life, your own haunts, where you will remain warm and comfortable.' Christ said: 'You will be a leaven, a leaven in the bread.' Just try to recover the leaven from the bread! And He said: 'You will be the salt put in the food.' Try again to remove the salt from the soup! Christ has said again: 'You will be a light' — not in a showcase, in the store window, but in the world! It is a troublesome thing to be the salt and to pour out yourself in the food, to be the leaven which loses itself in the bread, but it is the mystery of the Church."

It is only the Christian who can put in that leaven and bring forth that salt. He cannot do so by retiring from the world. He must strive, rather, to penetrate into the world in which he finds himself. He must make his presence felt there as a member of Christ, as another Christ, so that he might implant the truth of Christ in their midst. Bringing Christ to the world means that the Church must make its presence (*His* presence, which is the same thing) felt vitally, vividly, concretely, in those places where the real problems lie: in the office, the factory, the school, the home, the playground, the press, the battlefield, the theater.

The mystery of the Church, then, is the mystery of Christ living *in* His Church, living *in us:* Christ incarnate in those men and women who are His Mystical Body. What I have said, of course, is nothing more than an application of the doctrine of the Mystical Body to everyday life. That is the *leitmotiv* that keeps reappearing; the theme upon which the variations are built. I write of it with one special thought in mind. The Mystical Body of Christ upon earth is the Roman Catholic Church. The term "Christian society" is, as the

famed Cardinal Billot remarked, synonymous with "Catholic society."
I would not wish to mislead on that point. There is, I admit, a certain temptation to water things down a bit as I write. It might increase the number of readers if I were to talk about the "Christian
spirit" instead of the Catholic Church; and some of those readers
might then imbibe a few of the principles of Christ almost without
realizing it. But I cannot. I am overwhelmingly convinced that the
world needs more than a vague "Christian spirit." It needs the fullness of Christianity. For me, that means the Church. If I were to
eliminate the Church, my view of Christianity would wither away
before my very eyes.

"It is not a watered-down Christianity that holds the solution
for the world's ills," I have written later on, "and it is not the
flimsy substitute for the real thing that will ultimately draw men to
embrace the Christian way of life. The fullness of Christianity is
what the world needs: a Christian faith that includes a visible Church,
and a pope, and visible sacraments as the means of grace, and a
corporate act of worship called the Mass. This is the Christianity that
came from Christ, and that will save the world." I know no other
Christianity. What Christianity there is in the world apart from
the Mystical Body of Christ is still derived from that Church alone.

I hope that I do not seem to tread on others' toes. I have not
done so consciously, nor written in any spirit of ill will. I would
only want those outside the Church to see it as a Catholic sees it.
I could not even feel honest toward them if I clothed my real con-
victions with vague phrases that I know could never really satisfy
them, any more than they could satisfy me. They hear so many things
about the Church that are untrue; it is my hope that they might
gain here some insight into what it really is. If they see something of
that, they will know for themselves how wrong and prejudiced these
other viewpoints are.

The Scripture, the encyclicals of our modern pontiffs have offered
much in the way of inspiration toward understanding these truths.
But I found, also, that I returned time and again, as I wrote, to the
letters of Cardinal Suhard. Our modern world will seldom know a
more accurate and systematic appraisal of itself; the members of

the Church will rarely see such insight into the vocation that is theirs. Not always easy to read and comprehend, they are nevertheless rewarding.

I have quoted frequently from the papal encyclicals and from the letters of Cardinal Suhard because I think they should be better known, even among Catholics. This is especially true of the papal encyclicals. There have been some that are veritable masterpieces in a dozen different fields, and yet they are almost unknown in those circles where one would expect to find the most avid audience.

Possibly there is another reason for the frequent use at times of these troublesome quotation marks. Someone once remarked after reading something I had written, that I must be looked upon as somewhat radical or liberal in Catholic circles. He happened to be a non-Catholic, but some Catholics might think the same. The quotation marks, then, are a reminder to them that these views stem from the highest authorities in the Church, and not from some Christian malcontent. In fact, I find that I turned to use a quotation whenever it seemed that some particular statement *might* be pointed out as "radical." It was my way of saying that the doctrine of the Mystical Body, the need of the apostolate, the progress of the liturgy and social justice are only as "liberal" as the Supreme Pontiff. I would not wish to be less so.

* * *

I wish at this time to express appreciation to the Rev. Joseph J. Holleran, Archdiocesan Director of the Cana Conference for the Archdiocese of Milwaukee. His courses in Religion and Sociology at St. Francis Seminary were filled with practical applications of the doctrine of the Mystical Body, and many of them have found expression in the chapters which follow.

I would also like to thank the Rev. John T. Donovan, the Rev. Thomas D. Hickey, and the Rev. Florian J. Mac for their help and suggestions in preparing this book; and also the Rev. R. G. Simonitsch, C.S.C., whose review in *Worship* of an earlier book entitled *The Living Christ* first suggested the present volume.

CONTENTS

IN THE IMAGE OF CHRIST

CHAPTER I

TO LIVE IS CHRIST

I came that they may have life,
and have it more abundantly. . . .

OUTSIDE my window there are some children playing. They are playing those games that belong to the world of childhood; games that one generation has ever passed on to the next, explaining so carefully the little details that must never be set aside. Happiness is close at hand, and what the children seek is hiding now behind that next tree. They laugh and giggle and cry, and soon forget, and laugh again. And over in the carriage, their baby brother watches wide-eyed though speechless, gurgling his delight.

On the porch sit an aged grandmother and grandfather, watching these youngsters, but seeing themselves as they were so many years ago. At the end of life they see again the beginning of that journey, but now they see also all that comes between. They can hear the school bells ringing, the youngsters coming home with a book or two slung across their backs. They can hear the factory whistle blow, and watch for the fathers to return to their homes at the end of a busy day. They watch the truck drivers pass by, the doctors and salesmen, the butchers and plumbers come and go. Inside the house they can hear the mother busy with dishes and pans, preparing dinner, humming quietly as she goes about her work.

Across the street, they relive that unique experience of growing into manhood and womanhood. They smile at the cracking voice of a boy soprano fast becoming a tenor; they feel a bit wistful when they realize that the little girl next door is now a young lady. They return to youth again when they see the young couple passing by, so much in love; they go back to that age when each could see the whole world by gazing intently into the eyes of the other. And they remember how that love grows deeper with the years, with every child, with every sorrow, with every joy. They know the love of the present moment: the love that speaks more clearly by a presence than by words.

The whole of life stands there before them. Life — a puzzle, a riddle. What does it mean to live? What *is* "living"? It is not joy, and it is not sorrow; it is a generous blending of each. "That future, with its hopes and disappointments, its successes and its failures, its pleasures and its pains, its joys and its sorrows, is hidden from your eyes. You know that these elements are mingled in every life, and are to be expected in your own." They remember those words of the marriage ritual. And now they know. We will be happy, and we will be sad; we cannot escape.

"What is life?" A question asked a million times, and answered in a million ways. There is not a person alive who hasn't faced that question, even though he may not have put it in so many words. We probably answer it best by what we think, and what we do.

For some life is sheer drudgery. It is dying upon a rack of monotony. Work from morning to night, day in and day out, year after year, until work is swallowed up in death and inactivity. These are the people who say they have no time to think about life; they are too busy for such things. They must work to live. This one thought so consumes their mind that life itself becomes work and nothing more.

Other men have sought an escape from such drudgery. For them, life has become the pursuit of something glittering and gay. "Let us eat and drink for tomorrow we shall die." Everything else fades into nothingness; this alone is "living." Whatever else is done, is done only as an "interlude," marking time until the next chance to *live*.

In one case, it will be the passionate pursuit of the warmly physical. Life itself will be identified with sex. The first and last thought of the day, the constant companion of every hour, will be sex in some shape or fashion. "What else is there to life?" they ask. It fills our conversation, our magazines, our novels, our movies. Nothing escapes from it. Human love itself passes under attack, so much so that our sophisticated world equates it with animal passion, and can only smile when someone refers to the "sanctity" of marriage. But such "adult" society is no less pitiful, in the last analysis, than the calloused creatures who flaunt sex in a burlesque house. They are all trying to convince themselves that they have found "life," when they know very well they haven't.

There are a good many gutters, and just as many plush cocktail lounges, which bear testimony to the despair of those who have looked for life in a bottle. "Let us eat and drink for tomorrow we shall die. Tomorrow, life will be at an end; let us live, then, until death overtakes us. Let us eat and drink; that's living." But why is it that those who eat and drink the most are the very people who hope for death to take their "life" from them? Why is it that those who have gone out purposely to "taste of life," grow tired of its taste so soon? What is missing?

Perhaps it is money. There are not a few men who have made that their life. Everything they do revolves around that one concern; it is their "life." "Only the rich can live; the others only exist." The purpose of life, then, is to get rich; that must be our goal. We must have more money, and more diamonds, and bigger cars, and the most expensive clothes. Then we've gotten somewhere in life. Or have we?

Others have tried "success." Life means getting ahead, bringing other people to your feet, becoming "great." There are some people who even wonder if you *can* really "live" outside of Hollywood or New York. Perhaps they never stop to wonder, either, just why a good number of those who have achieved "success" will turn against it; if they have found the secret of life, why should they leave the plaudits of the crowd, push through the hordes of autograph seekers, and go home to take an overdose of sleeping pills, or put a bullet through their head?

The truth is, modern man is as much confused by the meaning of life as ever. Like men of all times and places, he looks for the answer in the most obvious things; he seeks the things closest at hand. Sex, drink, money, success. Or he accepts the inevitable: the purposeless drudgery of life, the monotony of work and toil, with no meaning, no reward.

It makes for interesting (though often alarming) discussion, this question of life. Try and sound out your friends, your relatives, your fellow workers. "What are you living for? What's life for anyway? Why are we here, what should we try to do?" It makes good discussion *if* you can get them to *discuss* it! The modern man has an unusual aversion to discussing such things intelligently, mostly because he feels self-conscious. And he feels self-conscious because usually he has never given the matter any real thought; he doesn't know what to say. A man might have memorized catechism answers in religion class a dozen times over, and still not have caught the real meaning. He might have heard certain truths in hundreds of sermons without those truths ever coming to life *for him.* That's why believers will stagger from bar to bar, arm in arm with those who have no faith; that's why they will buy their share of sex literature, and help to keep the cheapest road shows going. It is not all "weakness," by any means; it is more often a lack of conviction. When a man doesn't really grasp the full and true meaning of life, he readily accepts something else in its place.

In other words, we live in a pagan world. Because of that, we attempt to explain life on the only level a pagan knows: the physical and the material, all wrapped up in the present moment. Even the believer cannot escape this influence, unless he is awake to it. "We need not go far to find godless people," wrote Cardinal Suhard. "We meet them at every step. A great many baptized souls, while not actually atheists, nevertheless act as if they were. . . .

"True, a family spirit or custom leads them to perform certain seasonal acts of devotion, but do they possess a true faith? Is their piety not an empty formality? Proof of this can be seen in their actions. Their conduct does not differ from that of the nonbelievers among whom they live. They read the same books, take part in the same amusements, and share the same viewpoints on life in general and current events. Their spiritual poverty is particularly obvious in their concept of family life. Not only are they incredibly tolerant of divorce, companionate marriage, abortion and contraception, but at times they even advocate such evils."

Even concerning many practicing Catholics, he has this to say. While they "have not completely surrendered to materialism, [they] have to a great extent lost the understanding of what God is. Assistance at Sunday Mass and very often the reception of the Sacraments have become a sort of routine that they fall into. For them religion is a form of insurance, or a mark of good breeding. Religious duties are performed as though they were some necessary but tiresome formality requiring sacrifice on the same level as social conventions." It reminds us of the words of the priest quoted by Claire Bishop in her *France Alive:* "The religious factor occupies very little space in the life of the masses. . . . The proletariat is a pagan people with Christian superstitions. These superstitions are called baptism, First Communion, marriage, last rites."[1]

Are they too harsh? We can answer that best by taking a good look at ourselves and those about us. What do we see? There is an isolated star shining here and there, but the over-all view is none too bright. All about us we see men who have lost sight of the meaning of life; perhaps we see ourselves in their midst. Life has no greater meaning, no more lofty purpose than the pursuit of sex pleasure, the making of money, or the achievement of alcoholic oblivion. Even those who do catch some glimpse of the real meaning of life are likely to let the more obvious things blot it out.

Perhaps our biggest error is our failure to stand up and face life. There are not many who haven't, from time to time, caught some glimpse, however fleeting, of what life *really* means. But we try to avoid it; we try to escape from it because it seems so far away, so hard to reach. We settle, at those times, for what is near

---

[1] From *France Alive* by Claire Bishop, copyright 1947, by Declan X. McMullen Co., Inc., New York.

at hand. We more or less refuse to face life, to seek an answer to the puzzle it presents. We refuse to accept its challenge even when the fog of confusion lifts. And so the pattern goes on: work, drudgery, boredom, escape, sex, drink, money, success, frustration, despair. Life becomes a meaningless pursuit of phantoms.

After World War II, a circle of black-garbed "existentialists" began to gain great prominence in France. They are no doubt a passing fad, but they stand as a symbol of our age. These somber men and women have a philosophy of life, an explanation of life that reflects the modern spirit. They get their name from the word "exist." To live in the present, is all that matters; to make the most of the material things about us while we have a chance. Beyond them, life has no meaning; death closes all. That is why they speak so much of fear and dread. It is a fear born of the complete lack of meaning in human existence; a fear born of the utter lack of purpose in human life. Man flounders about the elements, looking in vain for help or consolation. He stands poised upon a hopeless pit of despair. Everything is dark, black. "The history of every man," writes Jean Paul Sartre, "is the history of a failure." The quintessence of our modern spirit.

What *is* life? Is there a better answer, a less terrifying one? There must be; and there is. To find it, we must turn our gaze back upon another age, more pagan, if possible, than our own. Into that void, a not very striking tentmaker from Tarsus issued his cry. Yet it was a cry that echoed back and forth from one corner of the Roman Empire to the next; a cry that overturned the futile world of the Roman gods.

CHAPTER II

THE VISION OF ST. PAUL

*I am the way, and the
truth, and the life. . . .*

THE Apostle Paul was a Roman by birth, "a Jew from Tarsus in Cilicia, a citizen of no insignificant city." As a member of the Hebrew race he possessed all the teachings and traditions of the chosen people; as a citizen of Tarsus he knew also the spirit and the culture of Greek and Roman civilization. But it was on the road to Damascus that he discovered another spirit, an over-all spirit that would unite both Jew and Gentile in a totally new way of life. He discovered the spirit of Christ. "If then any man is in Christ, he is a new creature; the former things have passed away; behold, they are made new!"

Life, in the eyes of St. Paul, is bathed in eternal and divine light. As for all true followers of our Lord, life takes on a new and unsuspected meaning with the coming of Revelation. St. Paul expressed it simply in these words: "For to me *to live is Christ!*" All of human life, all its meaning, is wrapped up in Christ. The purpose of life, the meaning of life, the goal of life is not to be found in those pleasures that are close at hand; it is to be found in Christ, and Him alone. Paul "determined not to know anything among you, except Jesus Christ and him crucified." In all about him he saw only the image of Christ, and he labored without ceasing that those whom the

Father had called might "become conformed to the image of his Son."

In order to bring this about, Christ became in all truth a member of our human race, "one tried as we are in all things except sin." He felt the cold and the rain; He knew, as we do, the sting of human sorrow and the warmth of human love. He made our world His own in a special way by becoming a *part* of it. Christ is not some far-distant proprietor who has claims upon the world. Christ is one of us. He trod our pathways and preached in our valleys and prayed upon our mountaintops. He is Emmanuel: God with us.

But there is more than that. Scripture points out to us a mystery that goes even further. When the Son of God humbled Himself to assume our nature, He was merely stooping down to lift us up. He made Himself one with us so that we, in turn, might become one with Him: that, as we pray each day, "we may be made partakers of the divinity of Him who vouchsafed to become partaker of our humanity, Jesus Christ Thy Son, our Lord." Christ would give to the Christian His life, His power; He would place them in the depths of our soul. He has turned over to us His goals and aspirations, His divine knowledge, His love — Faith, Hope, and Charity. We must share also His concerns. Because of this identity with Christ, our entire outlook on life is changed. "Have this mind in you which was also in Christ Jesus. . . ." The members of Christ can have no other! They are all *other Christs!*

Christianity, then, is something that "takes hold" of *us*. It is not simply a set of truths that we must accept; it is not simply a moral code outlining what we must avoid or what we must do. It involves vital contact with Christ, and inner union and oneness with the God-Man Himself. "Let us rejoice and give thanks," cries St. Augustine. "Not only have we become Christians, but *we have become Christ!*"

Until we reach these depths, we but touch the surface of our Christian way of life, of our life in the *Church*. For to our minds, the Church must be, as Bossuet expresses it, nothing other than *"Jesus Christ prolonged in space and time, and communicated to men."* Everything in the Church, and everyone in the Church is *Christ*. The human element takes on its real meaning from the enveloping glory of Christ. Thus, as Moehler phrases the same thought: "The Church is the Son of God Himself, everlastingly manifesting Himself among men in a human form, perpetually renewed, and eternally young — the permanent incarnation of the Son of God."

Owen Francis Dudley, the convert-priest, stands forth as a striking witness to this life of the Church. "I was told," he writes, "that the Catholic Church always placed the Church before Christ — that Christ was kept in the background. I have found, on the contrary, that she places me in a personal relationship with Christ that can never be attained outside — that Christ is her very being, by whom and for whom she exists, and to whom to unite her children is her one ceaseless care. . . . I was told that in the Catholic Church it was all decay and stagnation. I have found, however, the very life of God Himself pulsing through every vein of His Mystical Body. It was like coming out of a small stuffy room with all the windows closed, and striding up to the top of some great hill with all the winds of heaven roaring round. I have found Life."

In saying that the Church is Christ — that we people who *are* the Church, are Christ — we are reaching into the very heart of the mystery of our Christian faith. It is not a mere figure of speech and no more. The life of the Catholic is completely filled with Christ. "A Christian," writes Emile Mersch, "is someone who refuses to see anything else than Jesus Christ." Instead of seeing the Church as a *barrier* between himself and Christ, the true Christian sees *nothing but* Christ. He sees Christ in himself, and learns to cry out with St. Paul those terrifyingly beautiful words: "It is now no longer I that live, but Christ lives in me." And he sees Christ in others: "He is the bishop I obey; He is the sick child I nurse; He is the poor man I help, the youngster I teach, the people to whom I sell, the man with whom I work. It is Christ in all these others who gives them their greatest worth. It is Christ in my husband, my wife, my children; Christ in my friends and relatives, my fellow workers, the man across the street; Christ even in my enemies." As St. Augustine wrote so long ago about the ultimate goal of the Church's life: *"Et erit unus Christus amans seipsum . . .* and there shall be one Christ, loving Himself." Christ in His members, loving His members. One Christ knowing Himself, teaching Himself, sanctifying Himself, that Christ alone might be "all things and in all."

All of human history shares in this search for Christ. All wars, all cultures, all civilizations; all literature and art, science and industry are but a part of this gigantic struggle in which Christ seeks His fullness in mankind. As Cardinal Pie once remarked: "The history of humanity, the history of nations, of peace and of war and especially the history of the Church, is but the history of the life of Jesus filling all things."

What might seem to be a rather vague and meaningless statement is actually filled to overflowing with practical import. It is this fully "Christian" outlook that gives drive and meaning to our days. That is why Christianity is not just another way of thinking, nor a pious "hobby" that a man might take up or set down at will. The words of Christ contain the most basic truths in human life; and for that reason there exists a crying need for Christ's teaching in the modern world. There are many things in science and letters of which we could be quite ignorant, and still get along very well. But there is no man anywhere who is not harmed by a failure to understand *Christian* truth. Human life derives its full and complete meaning from that alone.

St. Paul knew how much men need Christ, and as he approached the pagan world of his day, he called out his solution with unmistakable clarity. "The night is far advanced; the day is at hand. Let us therefore lay aside the works of darkness, and put on the armor of light. Let us walk becomingly as in the day, not in revelry and drunkenness, not in debauchery and wantonness, not in strife and jealousy. But *put on the Lord Jesus Christ. . . .*"

Deep down within ourselves, we are a tremendous mystery. Left completely to ourselves, we live in conflict and turmoil, within and without; we long for what we do not have, and we reach out for what we cannot attain. Because of the conflicts we find in ourselves, our living seems to have lost its purpose. When we look into ourself, we cannot find the answer, no matter how piercing is our gaze. That answer must come from the *outside;* that answer is a *supernatural* answer. It is Christ, and Christ alone, who can shatter that mystery.

"He who walks in the darkness does not know where he goes. . . ."
Let modern man, or any man, seek to fathom life apart from Christ,
and he will fail. The conflicts of man will appear as monsters, his
longings will be the torture of Tantalus, his living will lead only to
purposeless despair. There *are* such things in our human life as "sin"
and "grace"; we possess *other facts* of human history apart from wars
and treaties: there is an "Incarnate God" and a "Redemption." These
belong to *history,* not to legend; and it is even more important for us
to know and understand these other facts of history than to know how
to plan an assembly line, or how to treat heart disease. Yet how many
thousands of men and women there are who, while they would never
underestimate the role of assembly lines and heart disease in modern
life, still treat grace, sin, and redemption as unimportant trifles or as
obsessions of religious fanatics.

Christianity, after all, is not something "extra" added on to the
world as an afterthought. It is, on the contrary, the center, the soul
of human life. It is the key for understanding the world and ourselves. We need Christ if life is ever to take on any real meaning.
Apart from Him, there is nothing but an endless chasm of despair.
No system of thought, no philosopher, no scientist, no social plan, no
manner of government can supply the answers which only Christianity
possesses.

Yet Christ's answers are not the moving forces in our day, and it
is not because He has not been heard. It is, rather, because He is now
ignored, rejected. The world goes on apace, and Christian ideals are
not playing the role that they should and *must* play, which is just
another way of saying that Christ is not having the influence upon
our daily life that He should rightfully have.

What Paul of Tarsus said in his days will hold true in our age,
as in all ages. The pagan spirit is not a thing that belongs only to
a part of history; it is found at every step. We can note something
special about that spirit in our day, however, as Cardinal Suhard did:
"In the Middle Ages, and even up to the nineteenth century, Christianity was localized on the planet, and the missionary apostolate
was geographical. Missionaries left Christendom to go and preach to
heathen nations. Paganism was *outside* the Christian world. Today, on

the contrary, the two cities are no longer outside each other but *one within the other* and closely interlaced. Pagan society penetrates everywhere the daily influence of Christians. At present, a closed Christian society, cut off from pagan influence, has become, it seems, unthinkable."

Our problem, in other words, is to *reconvert* a civilization that had once been, in large part, Christian. The men and women who walk our streets, who fill our offices and schools, who form our governments are very often people with "some" Christian ideas. What they need, however, is the *fullness* of Christ's word. Only too often, they have kept the phraseology and thrown away the spirit; and men who have absolutely no belief in God will speak quite glibly about our common need for "faith in the Divine." To lose God could only be described as a crisis for the Western World, because our way of life is rooted so firmly in Him. In one sense, the task of the present hour is even more difficult than that which faced St. Paul. Difficult as it is to convert a man to Christianity, it is even more difficult to bring men back to it when they have grown calloused and indifferent toward it.

Bringing Christ to the world will mean that His followers must make their presence felt vitally, vividly, concretely in those places where the real problems lie. Christians were never meant to do no more than gather in Gothic churches at regular intervals. Christianity is a total way of life, not simply a means of occupying a Sunday morning! Wherever any problems of our human life present themselves, there also must the Christian be present, to give the answer of God. There are influences at work in our civilization that are left untouched by any force that would Christianize them. There are men and women who live out their lives — lives often of great and widespread influence — quite apart from any spirit of Christ. There are professions in which the Christian spirit is not felt in any way that is personal and vital enough; there are whole segments of our modern life where men exist from day to day as though there were no Christ, no Christianity. It means something is wrong.

Christ did not come to set up some sort of "ghetto" Catholicism, where His members might retreat from the world. Yet it is an unfortunate fact, as Dorothy Day notes in giving her impression of

Catholics in the days before her conversion: "Catholics were a world apart, a people within a people, making little impression on the tremendous non-Catholic population of the country." It is not a heartening picture.

The follower of Christ cannot stand by idly and do no more than make note of the ills. He cannot be satisfied to have others solve the world's problems apart from the spirit of Christ. He must help bridge the gap between the false hopes of the world and its despair. He must bring to it the message of Christ. As a human being, composed of both body and soul, he must realize that saving souls must also involve such "worldly" topics as social reform, labor unions, family wage, the rights of ownership, medical morals, and the like. They are problems of the world. "The greatest error of the Christians of the twentieth century, and the one its children would not forgive them," warns Cardinal Suhard, "would be to let the world take shape and unite without them, without God — or against Him." As Christians, we could know no greater tragedy than this, no greater failure.

CHAPTER III

THE MISSION OF THE CHURCH

*I have compassion
on the multitudes....*

THROUGHOUT His entire life, Christ had compassion on the multitudes; His heart forever sought those who were in need. Nothing entered into the life of Christ more strikingly than His intense personal concern for the needs of others. It was a concern that touched upon the everyday realities of human life. He had compassion because "they have nothing to eat." His was a concern for the things of the soul, but He could not ignore the things of the body. Christ came to minister to human beings, not to angels; to individuals composed of body and soul, and not mere spirits. He must now continue to do that same thing in His mystical members. There is nothing more unChristian than a studied concern for "saving souls," coupled with a calloused indifference to man's very real material needs. It is unChristian because it is so unlike Christ, and so unlike His directions. He promised a heavenly reward not only because we pray for someone, or speak to a man of God's grace. He promised His reward also because: "I was hungry and you gave me to eat; I was thirsty and you gave me to drink; I was a stranger and you took me in; naked and you covered me; sick and you visited me; I was in prison and you came to me."

If Christ is to become truly alive in our modern world, He must become alive, really and truly, IN CHRISTIANS. If He is to live *among* us as He ought, it means living *in* us. When we say that Christian ideals and Christian truth will change the world, the Church reminds us that they will do so, *only* if they become alive in the men and women who are Christ's Mystical Body. That is their vocation. Ideas belong to people; they do not float about, suspended in mid-air like a magician's sword. Ideas must be clothed with reality. They must become something more, even, than mere words. If we do no more than repeat the teachings of Christ, puppet-fashion, throughout time, they will not change anything. They need to become a part of living people, and grow and develop in them. As Emile Mersch wrote of the doctrine of the Mystical Body, so also of the entire content of Catholic belief: "The world has need of finding it, not in books but in souls!"

Thus will Christ walk again the streets of our cities — in us; He will preach upon the mountaintop and within the valleys. Through His Mystical Body, His hands will again extend toward the poor and the needy and the homeless. Through those men and women who are His members, He will continue to go about doing good: healing the sick, defending the oppressed, rescuing souls for heaven. Through them His voice will continue to rise up in prayer, calling down upon troubled mankind the blessings and the peace of the Eternal Father. This is the mission of the visible Church: it is to represent the "permanent incarnation of the Son of God."

If any man asks of us: "Just what *is* a Christian to do?" the answer will not be difficult to find. He is to continue the work of Christ. A glance at the pages of Scripture will point out the way; it is this we want to talk about in the pages that follow. If at times certain men claim that the Church is interfering with questions that are none of her business, we can only say that Christ has led the way. If there was anything that Christ did, the members of His Body must do the same. If there was anything in which Christ expressed an interest, those men and women who are other Christs must direct their attention to that same field. What Christ began to do in time, He will not finish until eternity. What our Lord did one day on the slopes of Galilee or along the paths of Judea, He will continue to do in His members everywhere: in New York and London, Paris and Rome; in Bombay and Shanghai; along the Gold Coast of Africa and the ice-covered ways of Alaska; in Four Corners U.S.A., and in all the unnumbered crossroads of the world.

The follower of Christ must concern himself with the problems of society. This does not mean, of course, that the Church should be transformed into a sociological society. Its primary task *is* the saving of souls, and a Christianity that forgets this basic fact would be failing in its purpose. There must be a well-ordered concern. Yet we can hardly imagine our Lord walking through the tenement districts of our modern cities and contenting Himself with an impersonal remark about "How unfortunate it is that people must live under such conditions." Nor can His members remain aloof. They must continue to reflect the concern of Christ, a concern for souls that cannot ignore man's bodily needs.

Christ would not be satisfied with our paging through the books in our libraries, and laughing at the silly ideas these nonbelievers have about sociology; or what outlandish solutions they offer for our problems of crowded housing conditions. We will not displace their theories with our laughter. Only when the teachings of Christ are presented in *positive* fashion will men give up their erroneous beliefs. When next to their own books, there stand books written from the approach of Christ, we can hope for a change. When in the adjoining classroom the Christian solution is presented with as much fervor and scholarly detail as is the false, we may feel that we are doing what Christ would do. Laughter, silence, private condemnation, or public ridicule will not lessen the force of their arguments. It is not a negative attitude that we Christians must adopt, but a positive one. The believer must speak with as much clarity as the pagan, and with as much force, not content merely to tell others why they are wrong, but ready to give a definite solution with which to replace their views.

It will do the Christian world little good, for example, to condemn such evils as birth control, unless the members of Christ also take an active part in rooting out those economic and social reasons that bring on such practices. A man must have a large enough home in which to rear a family decently, and enough money to support them.

Realizing this, no Christian can see a family crowded into two or three rooms, with barely enough money for the present members, and feel that he has nothing more to do than condemn birth control. He cannot even be satisfied with pointing out such a partial, though at times legitimate, solution as the rhythm system. He has the further, more basic, obligation of doing what he can to bring about those economic and social changes that will make it possible for a God-fearing couple to be *able* to have the children they desire, and to support them properly.

Our Lord preached His doctrine of the oneness of mankind and the equality of each child of God. He would never walk down our streets today and note without comment the extremes of wealth and poverty that we find on all sides. Men may say that there have always been such extremes, even in very Christian countries and in very Christian times. Our only answer is that insofar as they allowed such conditions to exist, those times and places were less Christian.

Christ died to save all men; He looked upon them all as His brothers. Were He to come visibly into our midst once again today, we can easily imagine what He would have to say about our practices of race segregation. But according to His plan, we need *not* imagine it. He has left those men and women who are members of His Mystical Body to take His place. They are other Christs, and they must be His visible extension in time and space, speaking His mind, giving His solutions. A member of Christ who would refuse to sit next to a fellow member of Christ who happens to be of a different color, is in need of a closer look at Christian truth. Expediency is often given as the best argument for not pushing these changes too fast. Up to a point, it is a valid argument. But if men continue to use that argument and nothing more, is it really expediency? Or is it a refusal to live as Christians that masquerades under the name of "expediency"? For who are better fitted to lead the way in this regard than the members of Christ? If they hold back and are unconcerned, no one may make the break. Or if others do, their actions should surely bring a blush to the faces of these hesitant members of Christ.

The doctrine of the Mystical Body has been referred to as a doctrine packed with dynamite. And so it is. It is built upon the social nature of man, and the natural brotherhood of all human beings; but it perfects that natural oneness by supernaturalizing it. It intensifies that brotherhood by making all men brothers of Christ. It strengthens those natural bonds by adding new and more profound sources of oneness and unity. By making all men members of one Body, it has destroyed even the barriers of the Old Testament. "For all you who have been baptized into Christ, have put on Christ. There is neither Jew nor Greek; there is neither slave nor freeman; there is neither male nor female. For you are all one [person] in Christ Jesus" — the *Whole Christ*.

What our modern society has lost almost completely, and on so many levels, is a well-developed *social sense*. The individualism of the sixteenth and seventeenth centuries has tended to cut us off from one another. The social unrest upon which Communist philosophy depends so greatly, is based upon conflict between people. While men should work together, they actually tend to work against each other. The wounds of original sin keep making themselves evident in all we do. And once again, we find that grace comes to repair those wounds, and to perfect our human nature. The love of Christ comes to over-power the influence of Adam's sin, and to lead men on to new and undreamed-of heights. It is natural for man to be social-minded, even though he finds it difficult, in his present state, to live up to his own social ideals. But that is the gift of Christian faith. It brings to man that all-important grace which will enable him to achieve those ideals. And even more: through his faith, man discovers a new basis for his social ideals, a more perfect and a far more lofty reason for brotherhood. He learns of the unity of mankind to be fashioned "in Christ." He discovers that this natural social element in our human nature is destined to be raised up to something more; it is to be perfected in that divine oneness where we are all to be but "one person in Christ Jesus."

At the very rise of the Christian era, St. Paul put this social doctrine into practice. He wrote to Philemon about the slave Onesimus who had deserted his master, and whom Paul had converted to the faith: "Perhaps, indeed, he departed from thee for a short while so that thou mightest receive him forever, no longer as a slave, but instead of a slave as a *brother* most dear, especially to me, and how much more to thee, both in the flesh and in the Lord! If, therefore, thou dost count me as a partner, welcome him as thou wouldst me."

More "shocking" words could scarcely have been written at that time, so far as the pagans of the Roman Empire could see. No one but a true Christian could have penned them. Christianity, if it is lived fully, as it ought, will never become less shocking to the world. If the members of Christ do not cause such excitement, they might well examine their lives in terms of Christ. There is a world waiting to be refashioned. Our Lord did not come only to the men and women of His time; He came for all men, of all times and places. His followers do not simply "recall" His life. Rather, they enter into it: they *relive* it in themselves.

This is the Church: the extension of Christ — His Mystical Body. We need to see the Church in that light. "We must accustom ourselves," as Pius XII has written, "to see Christ Himself in the Church; we must strive to live in a spirit of lively faith . . . for it is Christ who lives in His Church, and through her teaches, governs, and sanctifies; it is Christ also who manifests Himself differently in different members of His society."

•Christ desires to wield His influence in our modern world no less than the world of the Caesars, and He will do this *through* His members. Any man can see how much depends upon the members of Christ living up to their obligations as Christians. Developing the true spirit of Christ, they must of necessity become tireless apostles. If they do not, the guilt lies upon the shoulders of each. Their fellow men depend upon their help to establish this vital contact with Christ; they cannot be indifferent to them. As other Christs, they can hardly keep from feeling, truly and deeply, a constant concern for others and their needs, for the betterment of the world: a concern that gnaws at their heart, urging them on to "re-establish all things in Christ."

When St. Paul wished to use a comparison to describe his very real concern for the Galatians, he could think of nothing more graphic than the suffering of a woman in childbirth. And yet that same Pauline spirit must flow through the Church today, filling the soul of every member of Christ's Mystical Body. Not content with merely being Christ in themselves, they must proclaim their concern to the entire world about them; they must look for the fashioning of a new world in Christ; they must cry out to one and all that they also, in the spirit of Paul, are "in labor again, until *Christ is formed in you!*"

CHAPTER IV

A CHRISTIAN WORLD

He who abides in me, and I in him,
he bears much fruit. . . .

WHEN a man begins to think about bringing Christ to the modern world, he is often overcome by the huge proportions of the task. We might easily enough think of religion as a little personal hobby that has few, if any, far-reaching consequences. We could be satisfied with trying to be as good as we can while remaining more or less indifferent to the rest of the world. It is not difficult to develop such an attitude in the world we know. Modern life is shot through and through with a spirit of independence: "What I do is my business; what he does, is his!"

Léon Bloy, in one of his anguished cries, gave voice to the feelings of many modern men and women: "I am dead drunk with sorrow, weariness, and terror! For more than sixty hours, now, practically all alone, I have been tending two sick little children and their mother — not eating, not sleeping, overwhelmed with sorrows, and without a penny. I am the anvil in the abyss, God's anvil at the bottom of the abyss! . . ."

"Practically all alone," he writes. Who cares? Who cares about him, his poverty, the sickness of his children and his wife? That is the modern spirit. The over-all spirit that reaches even into the hearts of Christians is often no more than the spirit of Cain. "Am I my brother's keeper?" Many a modern Christian is no less surprised than his pagan brother when he is told that the answer is and must be "Yes."

As soon as we begin to look about us, also, we become a bit more conscious of just how pagan modern life has grown. For those of us who have been trained in Christian attitudes since childhood, or who have turned to them as converts, there is a danger that we might fail to appreciate this fact completely. We might, on the one hand, move into our own little world and become "ghetto Catholics" — followers of Christ, that is, who overcome the world by leaving it entirely. Or, on the other hand, we might allow so much of the pagan spirit into our own lives that we even fail to see any difference. We could actually do so even without realizing it, and despite our Christian faith. We might be described as "compromise Christians."

The fact that we do get out of touch with reality is illustrated in a rather interesting fashion by the Catholic Action technique of the Jocists: "Observe, judge, act." The very first step demanded of these lay apostles is that they stop and find out just *what* the situation actually is. Looking at the matter superficially, it might seem impossible that men and women living in a definite set of circumstances could fail to understand those circumstances. Yet that is what happens. Often they have either become so engrossed in a ghetto life that they *miss* the problems outside of them; or, perhaps unwittingly, they have themselves absorbed so much of the false attitude that they *fail to recognize* some of their own positions as erroneous.

Christ did not come to set up a world of "ivory-tower" disciples. "I do not pray that thou take them out of the world," He said, "but that thou keep them from evil." And St. Paul said after Him: "I wrote to you in the letter not to associate with the immoral — not meaning, of course, the immoral of this world, or the covetous, or the greedy, or idolators; *otherwise you would have to leave the world.*" The disciples of Christ must mingle with those who do not have His spirit. They meet them in the market place; they face them across the bridge table, in factories, at movies, in schools, on the golf course. And if they must meet them, they must also understand them. They cannot run away.

The more subtle danger, however, is that the followers of Christ will mingle with others and still not see any noteworthy difference. Their daily lives will not be anti-Christian. There will always be a set of beliefs in the back of their minds — beliefs that they hold to firmly enough, but in a rather unreal sort of way. For all practical purposes, and without realizing it, their lives will be — like those of their nonbelieving neighbors — *un-Christian*. Their beliefs will not leave any distinctive stamp upon what they do; they will live in some sort of void. They are the Catholics of whom Cardinal Suhard was speaking: men for whom religion has become "a sort of routine . . . a form of insurance, or a mark of good breeding . . . some necessary but tiresome formality requiring sacrifice on the same level as social conventions."

For them, as for the modern pagan, daily life becomes dead monotony. They seek a world of escape. Work is a necessary evil, only to be forgotten in off hours. Working hours become only that time spent while waiting to continue the rituals of a smoke-filled cocktail lounge where the customers both noisily and quietly pass into oblivion. Family life is a thing of ancient history, exchanged now for the chilly banter of their drinking companions. The week-end drunk becomes the center of conversation, and, such as it is, a source of humor; a rather dubious "accomplishment" for which a man is cheered royally by his associates. Men and women are no longer persons but bodies; and the phrase "to make love" has no meaning beyond the grossly physical, utterly unexpressive of anything profound or spiritual. All entertainment follows the same pattern, and whatever reading a man does is such as would not be too disturbed by an aching head or a raucous jukebox. This is "living it up" in modern style.

It is not really difficult to live a Catholic life, if we actually try to *live* it. It is the compromising that makes it such a burden. If we once set out and begin to follow Christ completely, totally, unswervingly, we will find the road is not so trying as we had first thought. Christ will assume more of our weakness, and join it to His strength; we will find that His yoke is easy and His burden light, because He is with us and in us.

If, however, we try to be both Christian and pagan, religion becomes just something to talk about; not actually anything we try to live by.

Mass is what I missed last week, or what I will probably miss tomorrow if I don't go home now (followed by sophisticated chuckles). Confession is where I go in between "doing the town" and "hanging one on." It's best put off as long as possible, but it will get me temporarily in a state where I might receive Holy Communion. And prayer is what I do when I'm scared or need something awfully bad — contrition and petition.

It is hard to say just how many men and women could accept that as an apt description of their "Catholic lives." But they are, unfortunately, not a rarity. They are the untrained, unthinking, mechanical Catholics; the routine members of any church that claims to be Christian. Betty Smith touches upon such an attitude in *A Tree Grows in Brooklyn:* "Today the altar was lovely with banked scarlet poinsettias and fir boughs with the golden points of lighted slender white candles gleaming among the leaves. 'It's a beautiful religion,' she mused, 'and I wish I understood it more. No, I don't want to understand it all. Sometimes I say I don't believe in God. But I only say that when I'm mad at Him. . . . Because I do! I do! I believe in God and Jesus and Mary. I'm a bad Catholic because I miss Mass once in a while and I grumble when, at confession, I get a heavy penance for something I couldn't help doing. But good or bad, I am a Catholic and I'll never be anything else.' "[1]

As long as a Christian life remains on that level, it is futile to speak of "apostles." The individual's life must indicate a spark of something higher; there must be an all-consuming realization that these truths of religion are the most important facts of life; there must be a desire to understand our faith. Only then will there be complete, total dedication to Christ. Not that an apostle must be a saint before he can go to work! If that were true, the apostolate would be forever bogged down in the mire and never get started. But the apostle, be he layman, religious, or priest, must have this spark. There must be this spirit of dedication. It is a goodness of *striving,* but it must be a real and sincere striving toward personal holiness.

Some would look upon the task of Christianizing the world as a

---

[1] From *A Tree Grows in Brooklyn* by Betty Smith, copyright 1943, by Harper & Brothers, New York.

vast *technique* by which we overtake the world. They become involved in systems and plans, they engage in endless, often fitful, activities. They are "anxious and troubled about many things," and have little time or energy left for their own spiritual progress. We might, in a sense, compare Christianity to a world-shaking revolution, but its conquests are made in a manner far different from that of any other group. Its success or failure will depend not so much on the techniques the Christians use as the state of soul in which they use them. While the ideal is to have all things good, it can still be said that *good Christians* could convert the world faster with bad techniques than bad Christians with the very best of systematic planning.

We do not intend to dwell overmuch at present on the development of our personal spiritual life; we want to treat of the apostolic life. But we do want to stress the *absolute importance* of developing personal virtues; we want it taken for granted as an essential basis for all else we say. Without it, all else will lose its true meaning. St. Pius X, whose motto was "To restore all things in Christ," still emphasized this primary truth: "To restore all things in Christ by the apostolate of good works, divine grace is wanted, and the apostle does not get it unless he is one with Christ *When we have formed Jesus Christ in ourselves,* then *only* shall we be able to give Him easily to families and to societies. *All those who share in the apostolate must, then, have solid piety."* Of this we must *never* lose sight.

The Church would approach the work of the apostolate with two cautions in mind. In our strivings for economic and social reform, we must neither hope for too much nor too little. We must realize, first of all, that our hearts will never find complete happiness and rest upon this earth. We must echo the thought of St. Augustine: "Our hearts, O God, were made for Thee, and they shall not rest until they rest in Thee." An economic plan, or a sociologist's blueprint, that paints a picture of a Golden Age of unalloyed happiness, is most unreal. It will forever evade the grasp of fallen mankind. Even if we combine our hopes for reform with our search for God, we will never be 100 per cent successful; much less will we succeed if we attempt our reforms without God. The burden of Adam's sin will rest upon us until the end of time, as Leo XIII reminds us: "Man can no more make for himself a life devoid of sorrow and replete with unalloyed happiness than he can circumvent the design of God the Creator who has willed that the consequences of the ancient sin should remain until the end of the world."

This does not, however, mean despair, nor the refusal even to try to bring about reforms. The need for such changes still exists, and a large degree of success is possible. But the remembrance of Adam's fault will simply ward off the dangers of discouragement and frustration when our best of plans seem to go astray.

It is the Christian more than anyone else who can continue in these efforts without losing hope when he sees how much suffering and injustice remains. While he knows that man carries within himself the seeds of failure, he realizes, too, that — through the grace of God — he possesses the pledge of success. It is grace that makes possible whatever triumph man will know. For that reason, Leo XIII could also write that "It would seem impossible for the Church of Christ to contribute more to prosperous and happy living even if it had been born for the sole purpose of conferring or making more abundant the useful things and the conveniences of this mortal life."

We face a truly sad question in discussing these problems. "Why is it," we may ask, "that the very men who are most concerned and most zealous for an adequate solution, are those who have not been granted a Christian insight into the problem? And why do their modern solutions, arrived at apart from Christ, seem to be gaining the ascendancy in our present-day society?" It means that Christians are failing somewhere along the line. That is why the "generally accepted" doctrines and modes of acting in many fields today turn out to be those, quite frequently, which a Christian could not accept. The Catholic doctor, or lawyer, or worker is sometimes looked upon as a "foreigner" in his field; he has views that seem to fit in rather badly with some of the generally approved principles.

Certainly if Christians fail to exert their proper influence, others will solve the problems without them. The problems *must* receive an answer. But if these other men, despite their very real and deep sincerity, do not have the principles of Christ, their solutions may well be at variance with His. And if their solutions are the ones accepted, our modern spirit and manner of acting will hardly be those of Christ when they are put into practice.

The answer is not for the Christian to attempt to construct his own little world of medicine or law or labor relations or anything else; such an ivory-tower world would pass by the real, total world. He must, rather, penetrate into those very fields he sees about him, in which he finds himself. He must make his presence felt there as another Christ, to implant the truth of his divine Head. Missionaries and apostles are needed, not only in the African jungle, but on the crowded streets of our world capitals: apostles who will teach their fellow men the true meaning of life, repeating to them again and again that question of Paul: "Do you not know yourselves that Christ Jesus is in you?"

CHAPTER V

MARRIAGE IN CHRIST

Now Jesus too was invited to the marriage,
and also his disciples. . . .

ONE of the chief thoughts that we would emphasize is that the Church is a group of people. We must try to look upon it as more than a vague "something," all tied up with pictures of buildings and laws and Rome and bishops. Before there were ever any church buildings; before anyone even thought of a code of church law; before a single Christian appeared on the streets of Rome, and before a bishop ever wore a miter or a *cappa magna,* there was *The Church.* It was a group of people, some of whom were rulers and some of whom were the ruled over. But we must see them as a group of human beings, each one a real member of Christ's Mystical Body, and each one important in his own way, in the accomplishment of his own particular task. It is only in this way that we can see how each state of life enters into the total picture. And to see this social side of the Church, we must look to the beginning.

Human beings make their start in life in a family group; this is always the first and basic foundation of society. And the same is true of Christ's Church. There is a hymn by Katherine Tynan in the *New Westminster Hymnal* that expresses this thought:

Thy kingdom come; yea, bid it come —
But when Thy kingdom first began
On earth, Thy kingdom was a home,
A child, a woman, and a man.[1]

This will always be true. If Christ is to live in society, He must live first of all in this, the root of society; if He is to live in the world, He must begin His kingdom again, by living in the family.

In order to establish these first foundations of His kingdom upon earth Christ took what is most sacred and most noble on the human and natural level, and raised it to the level of the divine. He made it something supernatural. He took human love and marriage and made of it a sacrament; He made the family the birthplace of His mystical Body.

When the Son of God said through the prophet "my delights were to be with the children of men," He was simply giving expression to that tremendous love which burned in the heart of God for all men. The very spirit of love itself paved the way for this union of Christ and ourselves. The greatest longing of all love is to bridge the gap between ourselves and another, to break down the wall of separation between one individual and another. God loved us and came to us "and dwelt among us"; and His ardent prayer was that *"all* may be one, even as thou, Father, in me and I in thee . . . that they may be one, even as we are one: I in them and thou in me."

Because "He has loved us with an everlasting love," God sought to enlist even our human love in His work of redemption. Humanly speaking, it is marriage that comes the closest to that oneness, that unity we all desire; family life continues and enlarges that love. Because of that, it is only fitting that the Church of Christ, which is the Church of Love, should spring forth from the heart of the family. It is from this highest peak of human love and unity that this divine and supernatural union will take its rise. As human beings, we are all separate one from another; there is an inner loneliness rooted in the nature of men and women. Love seeks to leap beyond those boundaries, and thus in marriage, a man and woman pronounce a "voluntary and

---

[1] From *The New Westminster Hymnal,* copyright by Burns, Oates & Washburne, Ltd., London.

complete surrender of their individual lives, in the interest of that deeper and wider life which they are to have in common." The two shall become one flesh; and yet that alone is neither love nor marriage. The union of bodies is nothing unless it springs from something deeper. Physical union takes all its meaning from that deeper union of soul where, after giving up their individual lives, the man and woman become "one in mind, one in heart, one in affections." If this deeper bond is lacking, however, the physical union expresses nothing in reality. It becomes merely a burlesque of the most sacred role given to unaided human nature. Under such conditions, the act could never express this deeper union of mind and soul; and this is the only union it was ever intended to express. It is a meaning possible, moreover, only in that permanent state that arises when a man and woman promise each other to preserve this union of soul until death.

There can be no short-term love. Unless the gift of both man and woman is complete and irrevocable, and rooted in the soul, the giving is only partial. That is why not only the right, but also the very meaning of the sexual act follows upon the marriage; it can never really precede it. Sex apart from a permanent state of love may express a partial giving or a promised giving; it may indicate merely a surface emotion, or it may even conceal a lie, but in each case there is no depth of meaning.

Human love, in this way, is a beautiful thing when it is properly understood. The power of love which God grants to human beings is actually a share in His divine power; God shares with ordinary men and women His divine power of creation. To them He gives the power of bringing forth that human body into which He Himself will infuse a spiritual soul; He makes them co-creators with Himself. Having once created Adam and Eve, God decreed that He would no longer create men except through the instrumentality of those men and women who were to be their descendants.

It is the force and beauty of this God-given power that enhances the celibacy of the priesthood. As Father Trese writes when discussing why priests do not marry: "The procreative faculty is, then, outside the realm of grace, our most precious possession. We have not taken the vow of chastity because the power to propagate is a shameful thing, unworthy of a priest. We have taken our vow of chastity because in our love for God, we have been moved to offer to Him our *most treasured natural gift,* the one with which man is most loath to part — and therefore the one most worthy of the God Whom we profess to love with all the power of our being."[2]

Because of this deep sanctity of sex, we might expect that there is a further role involved in the instinct. A man and woman acquire the right to express their love physically only after they have divested themselves of their own individual lives; only after they have taken this gigantic step toward inner union with each other. And since this act naturally tends to the production of a child, the right is theirs only after they have also assumed an adult responsibility for those infant lives. Sex does not end with the bringing of a child into the world. The man and woman must realize that from the moment of the child's birth, their love is no longer merely something that they profess; it is henceforth something that *exists,* apart from them. They must see the child as the living embodiment of their love; they must direct that mutual love which is theirs to the training and care of the child. This takes time, of course; it takes a stable, permanent way of life. But that is why sex involves in its very essence the lasting obligation of family life.

All of this Christ came to tell to the world by His own example in Nazareth as well as by His teaching. He was born into a family group, and grew to manhood surrounded by the love of Mary and Joseph. His presence at the marriage feast of Cana so early in His public life might well indicate the importance of true love and stable families. It can tell us also where the work of promoting Christ's kingdom upon earth must begin. Should anyone ask what task Christ has given to good husbands and wives in the modern world, the answer is not difficult. Our neopagan world seems bent on destroying the sanctity of love and the permanence of marriage. No amount of preaching from the pulpit will overcome its error of itself. Modern man must see his mistake by *viewing* the real beauty and sanctity of marriage; by viewing the lives of those members of Christ's Church who have

---

[2] From *A Man Approved* by Leo J. Trese, copyright 1953, by Sheed and Ward, Inc., New York.

embraced that state. The modern pagan must hear these truths from his friends and relatives and fellow workers who are putting them into practice in their own lives; he must experience them by seeing the beauty of their lives. The voice of their example will strike more sharply than the words of the priest. The priest, as it happens, is a man whom the modern pagan carefully avoids; should he, by chance, hear him speak, his only response is a polite smile.

The greatest message these husbands and wives have to give to the world is that of the *sanctity of love,* but not merely human love; they must speak of divine love, for it is this kind of love that must shine in their eyes. It is futile to speak about Christian love without speaking, at the same time, of the *grace* of Christ; it is grace that makes love Christian. Many men and women, especially our "moderns," stand appalled at Catholic ideals concerning marriage; "How naïve can a man be?" they ask. "After all, human nature being what it is, and sex being what it is, how can *anyone* expect me to live up to *such* ideals! They ought to come down out of the clouds! Those are standards for the angels; we've got bodies!"

Actually, if it weren't for grace, the Catholic attitude toward marriage and sex would be *most* unreal, and perhaps sometimes we Catholics are at fault for not emphasizing that enough. We do teach it though. We say that no one can possibly hope to accept and attain our ideals in that regard unless he also understands our belief about God's grace; or the other way around, we say that without grace, no one *could* live up to the ideals we accept. There is a very good reason why a man would be confused by these ideals if he hears them, and is led to understand that he has nothing more to go on than the wavering strength he sees within himself. He knows his own weakness only too well, and would possibly be the first to agree with the Catholic teaching about original sin. Without grace, no man can long avoid a serious transgression against even the natural law, such as we find expressed in the Ten Commandments. And the laws of marriage belong, mostly, to that group. Because of this, we can never present our ideals toward marriage on a "purely natural" basis. Indeed, the ideals themselves belong there; they are the most "natural" interpretation of love and sex imaginable. But the keeping of those ideals demands something more, something far beyond us: the help of God called *grace*. And this, too, is part of the message that those "married in Christ" must bring to the world.

We can easily enough see, then, what a curiosity it is for a couple to accept the ideals of Catholic marriage and hope to live up to them without living full Catholic lives. The compromise Christian who takes only a halfhearted interest in his religious duties can hardly help but end up living a married life little different from that of a pagan. Not using the means of grace amounts to the same as not having them to use at all. The Catholic couple who more or less leave God out of the picture, or relegate Him to certain days of their life only, are asking for trouble — and perhaps failure.

As we said, as deep and close and intimate as love is on the human level, there is still a separation, a difference. There is always something lacking. While married love and family life come the closest to bridging that gap between human beings, there is always a struggle, made worse by the wounds of Adam's sin. It is this that makes it possible for those united so closely to hurt one another so deeply. And it is not in humanity that we must look for the remedy to that situation. As long as these wounds remain, they are liable to break forth at any moment, to destroy the beauty and harmony of love. Strange as it may seem, it is only in an even *deeper* union and love that this possibility can be lessened; it is only in a divine love that human love can be secured. We must never cease telling ourselves and the world in general this truth. Only in Christ and His supernatural love is our human love perfected. Even in marriage, the man and woman must learn to see the greatest worth of their partner, not in his or her own goodness, or lovableness. They must learn to see the *greatest* worth in the image of Christ present within each of their souls, within the souls of their children. It is here that their own natural virtues are secured and perfected.

For many minds, human love crowds God out of the picture. For the Christian, however, the light of Christ should cover all, and make that mutual love sparkle with a divine radiance. Such a *transformation* is possible only with love, never with lust. It is this Christian love that will enable a man and woman to live in such a way as not to destroy the image of Christ they see in one another. What passes so falsely for love in much of our present-day literature, movies, and plays could never know this light of Christ. It has no regard for spiritual values and the soul. It springs from no depths, it never reaches beyond the surface appeal.

Real love finds a new and even deeper foundation in Christ, and from Him it draws a new and more far-reaching strength and stability. A man who loves his wife "in Christ" does not pass over her own charms; a wife does not ignore her husband's natural qualities in searching out the image of Christ. Human love, even when supernaturalized, retains its human appeal. But both the husband and wife realize that of all the good and lovable and attractive qualities they perceive in one another, this image of Christ surpasses every one, but destroys none of them. It only enhances the beauty of the others. Indeed, there is no choice made between love and God. Real love finds its deepest meaning in God. It becomes the ladder by which a man and woman may walk through life hand in hand up to the fiery throne of Eternal Love Itself.

CHAPTER VI

THE FAMILY

And Jesus went down with Mary and Joseph
and came to Nazareth,
and was subject to them. . . .

IF LOVE builds a home, then it is only fitting that the Spirit of Love should dwell there continuously. That is the Christian ideal. As St. John Chrysostom advised: "Let your home be a little church where the Holy Spirit may dwell." The Church is a group of people, united to Christ; those people are no less the church when they leave the cathedral and return to their own homes. Christ must continue to live in them; every father and mother, every daughter and son must try to see Christ in himself, and Christ in those about him.

There is a real apostolate on this front. The truly Christian home is a far cry from the typically pagan home (or should we say "house"?) that we see on all sides today. Hidden away in some drawer we might discover a set of envelopes telling us that this family attends a church. If we don't dig that deeply, however, we might miss that fact. We might find pictures of Greek temples, calendars with naked movie stars, and a whole library of True Adventure stories. We see no indication in the furnishings, though, that *Christ* is *the* reality of their life; no hint that their hearts are bursting over with the realization that Christ has come to be the center of all. At most, we might discover a crucifix hidden in some obscure corner of a bedroom where the guests won't see it — sort of a symbol of the desire to "keep our religion to ourselves."

The family sits down to dinner and rises up again without a thought directed to the Giver of all good things; their conversation admits the word "God" or the name of "Christ" only as an expletive. In place of Christian love we find the chilly banter of sophisticated society. You could dim the lights and even pretend you were in the finest cocktail lounge in town. Everyone is wrapped up in a private shell; there is very little warmth. Real feelings are seldom expressed because sentiment embarrasses the suave man of the world. This is "home." It is not really surprising if Christ has a difficult time growing in His members in such a home; He can hardly help but feel somewhat out of place. Religion is something reserved for church, something associated with incense and stained-glass windows. Only religious fanatics try to drag it into the family life.

The fact remains, however, that Christ *did* take an interest in family life; He *did* live in a family group; He *did* have a message to give to the world on that particular point, a message both of word and example. That is why His followers must also take an interest in family life, and continue, both by word and example, to give His message to the world.

The Christian home must be a miniature of the home at Nazareth. The spirit of Christ must prevail there; He must live in each member as He lived in Mary and Joseph. If we want to learn to "see Christ in others," there is no better place to begin than in the home. Henri Bremond mentions somewhere the beautiful sight of the Christian father, standing over the crib and worshiping Christ present in his infant son. The baptized child is filled with the grace of Christ, and His image there is unstained by any sin. Yet we must seek the image of Christ in all the members of the family, even though the passing years may know sin and failure. Even the soul of the "black sheep" who resists the grace of Christ remains sealed with the sign of Christ; by the character of baptism, His image remains imprinted, and we must seek that image. That is Christian love: loving Christ in others.

It is, of course, the mother and father who set the pattern for the home. They must first of all strive to see Christ in each other, and

they must give *evidence* of that deep love in the home. Love is nothing
to be ashamed of, and when it is sanctified in Christ, it becomes something holy, sacred. Even on the merely natural level, one of the greatest
benefits a child can derive from his parents is a living appreciation
of the beauty of human love. It will do our children little good to
hear nice sermons on the sacredness of love, or to read pious books
about it, unless they can *see* it for themselves. The young boy or girl
will draw the deepest impressions from their first contact with love,
and that is in the home. Those impressions remain the strongest forever. If he grows up in a home where the mother and father freely
express a sacred love for each other, the child will not be so likely
to think of sex as degrading and unholy. When, later in life, he
gradually learns more of the physical side of love, it will appear
natural, rather than shocking, that two people who obviously love
each other as mother and father do, should tend to express that love
as God intended. A surprisingly large percentage of warped and
perverted notions concerning sex can be traced back to homes where
human love was treated as something God tolerates rather than
sanctifies.

Such Christian love between father and mother takes for granted,
then, a highest regard for the soul of each. Their way to heaven is
through marriage. If they reach that goal, it will only be by remaining
faithful to their state of life, doing all they can to keep alive this
image of Christ within their souls. Sin, for that reason, becomes not
a purely private affair. Its social element is more apparent, for if sin
destroys the beauty of that love, a truly Christian atmosphere cannot
be maintained in the home. Perhaps it is another way of saying that
the first duty of every parent is to strive to become a saint. The truth
is that no Christian in any state of life can long succeed in playing
the role of a hypocrite. Sinful parents cannot bring about a truly
Christian spirit in the home. The conflict between what they say and
what they do will eventually become apparent, and from then on
their words will have little real meaning. It was for this that Christ
saved His sharpest words: the hypocrisy of the Scribes and Pharisees.
"But do not act according to their words; for they talk but do nothing."

Both father and mother, then, must let the image of Christ shine forth in all they do. They are the first persons with whom the child comes in close contact, and it should be through them also that the child first comes in contact with Christ. In their love, he should be led to see the love of Christ; in their generosity, their protectiveness, the generosity and protectiveness of God.

In addition, the parents must accustom themselves to seeing Christ in their children, ever anxious to build up that divine image within their souls. Apart from the peculiar talents, the special attraction of each child, there is this common and greatest worth: oneness with Christ. It is this especially that will help troubled parents to keep up their courage when their children disappoint them — giving them courage to be patient, to return time and again to repair the wrong, and put the child on the right road again. It is to their care, as Pius XII remarks, that "our Saviour has entrusted the youngest members of His Mystical Body." The performance of that office will many times demand the patience of Job and the forgiving love of the prodigal son's father. It is a lifelong task, and a difficult one, yet one that ranks clearly among the most important in the entire Church.

In order that Christ might live more fully in the home, the family should above all strive to follow the pattern of the Church year. It is this spirit of the liturgy that can best serve as a bond between the parish church and the home. What the Christian community is celebrating at any particular time should be continued within the smaller family group. Doing this, of course, means that the family will have to be fairly well grounded in Catholic teaching first of all. The home must be a place where religion is treated as an everyday *reality*. A realization of just what these truths mean is of far more importance than a knowledge of theological subtleties; the home is not a department of the university. But the atmosphere must be one in which such basic truths as original sin, grace, redemption, and union with Christ through the Church are understood in a very real way.

When there is such a deep grasp of the faith, different liturgical practices can easily be introduced into the home. Without such preparation, however, the end result might be ludicrous. The Advent wreath, to cite one instance, is a beautiful custom when it helps the family experience the ageless longing for the coming of Christ. When it is suddenly introduced into an otherwise "modern" family, however, the members most often experience a bit of embarrassment. They almost feel as though they have been abruptly introduced into some occult rite of a Buddhist temple. Even apart from that, any religious practice that is carried on without a deeper grasp of the doctrine it signifies will tend to deteriorate into something like superstition.

Granted a home atmosphere where these Christian truths are regarded as most important, Christ can live again most beautifully the life He passed upon this earth. He will live that life in the members of the family. The furnishings of the home, like those of a church, can build a fitting background for that life. The utterly profane would naturally be excluded. In its place there could be one or another truly artistic statue or picture, occupying a prominent place in the home. It should be something of which the family could be proud — not necessarily expensive, but well chosen. At least it should be something more than the cheap, emotional type of picture or statue too often featured by church-goods stores — pictures that shine in the dark, statues with movable glass eyes, and the like: what Archbishop Cushing described so well as "pious rubbish and religious junk: an insult to a Catholic's intelligence, and a waste of his money."

The spirit of the home — which is far more important — should be one that makes prayer easy; and the prayer should be a common prayer at times, a social prayer. The Church is a group of people, a social body. This is true of the home also, for the family *is* the Church; and this miniature of the Mystical Body of Christ should pray often as a social body. Prayers at certain times of the day, prayers proper to special seasons of the year, the daily rosary, prayers before and after meals; all of these can fit into the daily life of the family with no great expenditure of time.

Certain feasts, often overlooked, should be celebrated as well. Baptismal days, the feasts of the different patron saints deserve some special notice at dinner, for example. Perhaps the baptismal candle could be kept to be burned only on that day; or a special place set for the child or parent whose patron feast is being commemorated.

Even regular family customs can be "baptized" as it were. To the Christmas tree there might be added the star of Bethlehem and a crib. Easter eggs might be decorated with different symbols of the Church year, as one writer suggests, printing "Alleluia" on only one egg, and letting the children regard it as a special honor to find that egg. Cakes might be decorated with symbols of the faith, and certain dishes associated particularly with one or another big feast. Candles from the Easter Vigil might be burned again at the Easter meal.

Over all, however, the spirit of the particular season should prevail in the home. In Advent, there should be an atmosphere of hushed expectancy, awaiting the coming of the Infant King; the Advent wreath could help in that. Christmas should be a time filled with the happiness of Christ's gift of Himself — the greatest Gift of all those received. Epiphany should continue that spirit, and emphasize also the apostolic spirit, the desire to spread the good news of Christ far and wide among all nations.

Lent can be a time of penance in the home, penance undertaken by one and all in a spirit of love, rather than an empty, cold mortification. Even the youngest child could add his little bit, and the entire family should encourage one another in their good resolves. In that way, Christ will live His Passion and death in the family, and every member will feel the triumphant joy of Easter morning. On that day, all will feel that not only Christ, but they themselves have overcome the power of Satan, and risen to a new and higher life.

The days from Ascension Thursday until Pentecost Sunday should be a repetition of those days of anxious waiting in the upper room; like the Apostles, the family should make its own novena to the Holy Spirit. Entered into in that spirit, the season of Pentecost can become a season of spiritual growth, lasting throughout the long summer months.

If our lives are lived according to that spirit, day after day, we cannot help but become more like Christ; we cannot help but seek the strength of the sacraments with ever increasing frequency. That is the very purpose of the sacred liturgy: "it strives to make all believers take their part in the mysteries of Jesus Christ, so that the divine Head of the Mystical Body may live in all the members with the fullness of His holiness." And it is in the family group that He would begin that mystic life.

CHAPTER VII

THE VICAR OF CHRIST

*And I will give thee the
keys of the kingdom of heaven. . . .*

CHRIST came to this earth with a mission to fulfill; He came as one sent by another, with a task to accomplish. Scarcely had He begun His public life when the Jews were astonished at His teaching, "for he was teaching them as one having *authority."* And He Himself said: "All power in heaven and on earth has been given to me."

Because of this, His Church must also possess authority. If the life of Christ is to be continued through His members, this power which was His must be ever present as well. A Christianity without authority makes as much sense as would a Christ without authority. Christ did not come to our world simply to utter opinions; He came to proclaim the unchanging truth. He came to lay the yoke of His law upon the shoulders of mankind; He came to rule over our minds and our hearts. And since this was so important an element in the character of Christ, He could not really live on in His members, unless He was able to go on living and teaching through them "as one having authority."

Christ does this through His bishops, the successors of the Apostles; He does it chiefly through the bishop of Rome — through Peter, the Prince of the Apostles. Undoubtedly Christ dwells no more strikingly in any of His members than in His Vicar in Rome. Christ is so intimately united to the Holy Father in his *office* and his *official* capacity, that they form but one unit and they act as though one person. What is true of all of Christ's members is eminently true of the visible head of His Mystical Body: he is *one* with the Redeemer. St. Catherine of Siena understood this well; when speaking of the Holy Father, she always referred to him as "dear Christ upon earth."

The roots of this identification with Christ spring from the official position of the Holy Father. Certainly this official oneness should be matched, as far as possible, by an intimate union of soul; the lofty honor of Roman Pontiff carries with it the serious obligation of personal sanctity. Yet failure in that regard could not destroy this official oneness with Christ. Even in the years of its decadence, the members of Christ could still look to the papacy and see there the image of Christ. No historical study of the personal failure of any pope would even touch upon this point. Christ established His Church with His divine power; He did not leave it to depend upon the vacillations of any human will.

In the same way, we must learn to see Christ and His authority in our bishops. What the pope is to the universal Church, each individual bishop is to his own diocese. "They are united by a very special bond to the divine Head of the whole Body and are rightly called 'principal parts of the members of the Lord.'" The men and women who form Christ's Church in one particular diocese "are ruled by Jesus Christ through the voice of their respective Bishops." Christ lives in them, therefore, in a most striking fashion, and it is because of that singular image that Christians throughout the world give special reverence to these bishops. The natural talents of one or another man might enhance the respect given him; his administrative ability, his pleasing personality, his power of oratory, his intellectual brilliance. However, should a man be entirely lacking in these, the basic reason for granting reverence to him would remain. Even should the man be possessed of a hideous temper, a most unpleasing personality, he would deserve the respect of his office; in him we can still see Christ — an image that does not come from his own natural talents or personal virtues, and that cannot be effaced by lack of them.

The need to perpetuate the ruling power of Christ in His Mystical

Body springs also from the nature of this Body. We are dealing with a metaphor; Christ chose to perpetuate His life, not in another physical body, but in a group of *people*. Together they would fashion His Mystical Body, the Church. But if you are to join a group of human beings together for any purpose whatsoever, you must have a ruling power. Man is by nature a social being; he is not simply a gregarious animal. There is a difference. Animals follow the herd by instinct, but social activity on the part of man depends upon the right use of his intellect and free will. It is, of course, natural for man to *choose* to live with others and to work with them; yet that very choice comes from his free will rather than blind instinct. A mother bear watches over her young because instinct prompts her to do so; a human being adds to her motherly instincts the peculiarly human trait of *love* — something of which only an intelligent creature is capable.

As human beings, then, we simply must seek the help of others in doing what we would want in this life. We all have certain needs which can only be met by the co-operation of our fellow men. We are born into a family group, where we will be housed and fed and protected until we are old enough to set out alone. We depend upon the help of others in acquiring our education. We band together with other men in order to work or to seek recreation; we join forces with others to find a common protection in time of war; we associate ourselves with other men in political life in order to achieve the interests of peace. There is nothing we do that we do completely alone.

It was not surprising that Christ should have chosen to make our salvation share in this social pattern as well. As we said before, He did not *have* to do so; He willed to help us reach heaven in this way so that "all might co-operate with Him in dispensing the graces of Redemption," as Pius XII remarks. It is a part of God's plan "to re-establish all things in Christ"; to make all mankind "one person in Christ Jesus." Yet, establishing such a social body would necessarily mean that there would be rulers and ruled. A family must have a father; a government must have a president or a king; an army must have a general. And a Church must have a ruler.

Even more, since the Church of Christ will deal with *supernatural* truths — truths which man can neither learn nor understand apart from God — the rulers of the Church must possess certain divine helps. They are the ones who must lead; they must have some assurance that they will go in the right direction. They are the ones who will be asked a multitude of questions about these supernatural truths; they must know for sure that their answers will not be in error. That is what Christ meant when He promised that "the gates of hell shall not prevail against my Church." That is what Christ meant when He said to Peter: "Simon, I have prayed for thee, that thy faith may not fail; and do thou, when once thou hast turned again, strengthen thy brethren." The Church is a group of people who adhere to supernatural truths; a leader in that group would be no leader at all if he could not point out the way, and give the correct answers. To say that Christ promised to make His Church indefectible, means simply that He promised this divine help. When we say that the pope or the assembly of bishops throughout the world are infallible, we mean only that Christ is keeping His promise: He holds them back from error when they give their final answers on matters of faith or morals.

We can see how essential this idea of authority is to the Church, if we look at what happens when groups of Christians decide to eliminate the rulers. This was one of the chief goals of the Protestant Reformation: a church without "ministers"; or what amounts to the same thing, a church in which everyone was his own minister. With the passing of the years, however, the basic need of any social group for leaders has evidenced itself in Protestantism once again. The return to usage of such terms as "bishop," or the reintroduction of liturgical robes, and the wearing of Roman collars by the Protestant clergy indicate something far deeper than merely accidental changes. They emphasize the setting off of the ministers of the Gospel as a class apart.

In matters of actual belief, the situation does differ. There are today those groups of Protestants in which the word of the minister has all the authority of an infallible pope even though no such claim is made; but there are also the groups of Liberal Protestants who have realized that apart from a divinely aided authority, supernatural truths cannot be retained. They have rejected, accordingly, the idea of supernatural truth entirely. The early attempt to ascribe infallibility to a book, the Bible, spelled its own defeat; the endless round of interpretations as to just what the written word actually meant led only to endless confusion. The only other alternatives would seem to be either an authoritative *teacher* of supernatural truth, or the entire *denial* of all supernatural truth; either Dogmatic Protestantism (with little freedom) or Liberal Protestantism (with little faith).

Actually the beauty of Christ living in His Church extends even to the concept of authority. Others have claimed falsely that such a concept destroys the beauty of Christianity; in reality it enhances it. It is the pledge of Christ's security — of Christian security. "This he has done that we may be now no longer children, tossed to and fro and carried about by every wind of doctrine devised in the wickedness of men, in craftiness, according to the wiles of error. Rather are we to practice the truth in love, and so grow up in all things in him who is the head, Christ." So speaks St. Paul.

In forming the Church, and giving it a pope and bishops, Christ brought security into the way of faith. Until the end of time, Christ's definitive voice will ring throughout the earth. When men are confused and seek the faith of Christ in vain; when the discords of religious belief mount by the hour; when the flame of Christian light appears to dwindle, then will men cry out, like Pilate: "What is truth?" And Christ will answer loud and clear. Christ ever living in His Church will reaffirm the faith, and scatter the confusion; through these leaders and teachers of His Mystical Body He will hold high the torch of Christian truth, and surmount the discords raging on all sides. And when men cry out: "What must I do?" a human voice, that is yet the voice of Christ, will answer — an answer that is not an opinion, nor a probable interpretation: that voice will utter the divinely guided, unchanging truth. Those words will bear the seal of heaven.

Christianity is not simply the passing down of a dead, lifeless set of truths from one generation to another; it is a vital, living thing. To follow Christ does not mean to attempt to dress twentieth-century men in first-century garb. There must be growth, development. The truth that never changes must be adapted to the times which do. We must never change in the slightest the doctrine that is taught, but we can, we even must, adapt that doctrine to the ever changing world. Christianity must not be labeled "medieval" by our modern brethren. Yet if that is to be the life, the purpose of the Church, we see again the need of an ever present guide: a living, ever present authority that can decide once and for all just what is legitimate, just what is an adaptation in doctrine and what is a complete change. It is a tricky business. Doctrinal progress without a final court of appeals here on earth leads only to Modernism; and Modernism means only an ever changing belief: it means destruction of doctrine rather than development.

Pope Pius XII has pointed out this need. Teachers of doctrine, he says, "must so express themselves, in their spoken words as well as in their writings, that the men of our times understand and listen to them." But the first step in any such apostolate is to study the current conditions in the world that must be re-Christianized. Only after seeing both the present-day world and the doctrine of our Lord can Christians unite the two. Christ not only seeks to give His message through His members; far more, He wants those members to *integrate* that message into their own world, to make it a part of each succeeding age. Doing that demands thought; it demands guidance. It is easy to see how far the members of Christ could get from the true meaning of His doctrine, had He not given to certain men within that Church the power of speaking with His authority. Through them, He guides and limits and protects this progress. The Church does not enslave the minds of its members. Rather, through continuing the guidance of its divine Teacher, it opens the way for even greater progress. A man is not less free intellectually if he has a good teacher pointing out the right direction; he loses neither his dignity nor his freedom if he listens to that teacher's warnings about the blind alleys which lie ahead. And never are such warnings more needed than when a man is dealing with supernatural truth: when he is traveling down a roadway that must ever remain somewhat obscure to human understanding.

As Emile Mersch remarked: "A Christian is someone who refuses to see anything else than Jesus Christ. His docility to the bishops is the same as his docility to the pope, for it is the docility he has to

Christ." As long as we do not see Christ in our superiors, we do not see their right to command; it is through His bishops and His pope that the authority of Christ is mirrored in His Church. Through them Christ rules. "The hierarchy is not only the visible authority exteriorly comparable to the other human powers one observes in her," writes Cardinal Suhard. "It is a 'mystery' like the Church itself." To see Christ in others means especially seeing Him and His authority in the leaders of His Mystical Body. It is a mystery that has been grasped by centuries of devout believers. They have seen Christ present in superiors to lead them; they have seen Christ present in themselves as well. "Rome has spoken; the question is settled!" To the members of Christ these words mean nothing else but that "*Christ* has spoken; the question is settled!" It is a part of that deep and unfathomable *mystery* of Christ and His Church, of Christ *in* His Church.

CHAPTER VIII

THE PRIESTHOOD

I am the good shepherd, and
I know mine and mine know me. . . .

WHILE Christ spent a great portion of His public life preaching to large groups of people, He did not always act on a grand scale. There *were* the large numbers, the "huge" miracles like the multiplication of the loaves, the triumphant procession into Jerusalem on Palm Sunday. But perhaps the most characteristic picture of Christ in the believer's mind is something far more personal. He sees Christ walking over to the sick woman to give her health; he sees Mary Magdalen kneeling at the feet of Christ, the little children lifted up in His arms. Christ went about doing good, but, being God, He could always see the individuals with whom He was dealing. "In the crib, on the cross, in the unending glory of the Father, Christ has all the members of the Church present before Him and united to Him in a much clearer and more loving manner than that of a mother who clasps her child to her breast, or than that with which a man knows and loves himself."

In a similar manner Christ must continue to make His love felt in as *personal* a manner today through His Church. And it falls to the lot of His priests to bring that about. By virtue of the sacrament they have received and the commission they have been given, His priests are able to continue the ministrations of Christ. Until the end of time, they especially will make this personal concern of Christ for all mankind live on in the world. The priest will be "another Christ" in a most gratifying manner; he will be a true "pastor": the shepherd of souls.

Certainly Christ lives on in His bishops in a most special way; they are officially *the* shepherds of His flock. But all bishops, like St. Paul, must, of necessity, concern themselves with things on a broader scale; they are involved in what we call "administrative" duties. Unlike Christ, they cannot at the same time see each individual; they can see their flock only as a whole. Their vision must be forever broadened so as to include the entire picture at all times. St. Paul had that vision. Over and above all his sufferings and trials, "there is my daily pressing anxiety, the care of all the churches!" With so many problems on all sides, he could not possibly attend to every detail; no bishop can. They cannot rule over their flocks without help; they alone cannot attend to the instruction of their people, nor baptize them all, nor hear their confessions. They have need of assistance; they need their priests.

We can best understand the priesthood if we understand it in terms of the episcopacy. It is the priest who will "personalize" the concern of the bishop. Christ dwells in His priests as in His bishops, for they share the labors of the bishop. The priestly state flows from that of the bishop, the successor of the Apostles; the priestly office comes, in that way, from the Apostles themselves, who first shared their responsibilities with others. "The priesthood consists essentially," writes Canon Masure, "in a subordinate participation in the religious and apostolic functions of the bishop. The priestly state should be referred to the episcopal state not only as a part to the whole, but as the subordinate and the dependent to the principal power. Whatever the bishop does in a perfect, absolute, and independent manner is done by the priest in an imperfect manner, limited in time, in space and in power."

Yet the priest is not merely a powerless juridical appointee, taking the place of the bishop; not a mere "helper." He is, rather, a man who actually possesses a true, spiritual power — a man to whom Christ, acting through the ordaining bishop, has confided the very power of celebrating Holy Mass, of forgiving sins, of officiating at weddings, of helping the dying. The priest is a man whom the bishop may permit to preach in his name, and give to his flock, day by day, the everlasting truth of the Gospels. It is to his priests that the bishop entrusts the care of his parishes, his schools, his institutions. They are his "dearly beloved sons, chosen by our brethren to be our helpers in the ministry," as he says on the day of ordination. God gave to the high priests of the Old Testament "men of lower rank and inferior dignity, to be at their side and to assist them in their work." And in the same way, He "joined to the Apostles . . . teachers of the faith; and with their help, they have filled the whole world with the glad tidings of the Gospel." It is after considering this that the ordaining bishop thinks of his own needs and prays: "Give to us also such help in our infirmity; we need it so much more than [the ancient Fathers and the Apostles], as our weakness is so much greater. We beseech Thee, Almighty Father, invest these Thy servants with the dignity of the priesthood . . . may they be watchful fellow laborers of our Order. . . .": *Providi cooperatores ordinis nostri.*

With this in mind the bishop, at the beginning of the ordination ceremony, instructs those to be ordained: "Endeavor to be such that, by the grace of God, you may be chosen as helpers of Moses and the Twelve Apostles, that is, the Catholic Bishops who are signified by Moses and the Twelve Apostles." The priesthood finds all its meaning and its purpose in the episcopacy. A bishop is not a priest who happens to be raised to the fullness of the priesthood; the other way around, a priest is a minister who shares in the work of the bishop. Quite often the bishop is looked upon as no more than a ruler, an administrator. Yet as Cardinal Suhard remarks, "he is not only a leader who gives orders, controls things or reprimands; he is the symbol and the source of unity and life." Because of this, it is always his *priestliness* that deserves the first place, for it is this which seeks a fuller expression through those "dearly beloved sons, chosen by our brethren to be our helpers in the ministry."

This priestly zeal naturally seeks to express itself in the spiritual activity of the priest. While other members will mirror one or another interest and concern of Christ in the Church, the singular task of the priest is to perpetuate Christ's concern for spiritual growth. The *primary* purpose of a group within the Church called "priests" is to promote the spiritual development of the other members. Their life is a life dedicated to that ideal. A man or a woman becomes a religious to give greater glory to God, and to secure his or her own salvation. No one becomes a priest primarily for himself, however, but for others; the sacrament of Holy Orders is a *social* sacrament.

The priest, as a result, has need of many virtues if he is to perform his task well. But there are two qualities that must especially mark the life of a good priest. They have been singled out as a *sense of consecration, of dedication,* and *accessibility.*

The first is something involved in the sacrament of Holy Orders itself. A priest is a man set apart; he no longer belongs to anyone, not even to himself: he belongs to God alone. And yet, at the same time, he is not "out" of the world; he is very much concerned with the world: it is to save the world that he must give it up in part. He cannot consecrate the world and rid it of the conflict between God and self until he has first accomplished that consecration within the confines of his own soul. "For them I sanctify myself," he will say with Christ. His striving for holiness is something apostolic, something social. The priesthood exists for others, and a man must feel dedicated to that ideal. He must be willing and anxious, like Paul, to give his life for the good of his fellow men: "I will most gladly spend and be spent myself for your souls, even though, loving you more, I be loved less."

The world does not always look upon such dedication with a kindly eye. To many, the priest is a symbol of another world and another way of life that they have rejected. That is why the priest is persecuted; that is why angry eyes follow him down the street. He is a constant reminder of Christ, more perhaps than any member of Christ's Body. Yet he labors for all men regardless; he has the interest of every individual at heart. In the parable of the Good Shepherd, Christ set the pattern for His priests. They must be consumed with a love for souls. They must repeatedly go out in search of the lost sheep; they must stand between the world and their flock; they must, if need be, lay down their lives for their sheep.

It would be easier, no doubt, if the priest lost his humanity in assuming the priesthood; then his sanctity might not demand a struggle. Actually, Cardinal Suhard reminds us, "though we may rightly speak of the priest's sanctity, it is with reference to a sanctity in the making; a striving for sanctity, virtue in combat." His first task is to overcome his own human weakness. Yet this helps him to lead the way. When the other members of the Church realize this, they will be conscious of a stronger bond of humanity between themselves and their priests; they will strive hand in hand to imitate Christ their common Head. "Taken from among men," and "appointed for men in the things pertaining to God," the priest must, because of the obligations of his office, become "from the heart a pattern to the flock." He does not merely direct men in their quest for sanctity; he leads the way. The sanctity of his office demands that he himself seek holiness. He has no other choice.

To lead men, in this way, to the heights of sanctity, the priest must also make himself *accessible*. It will do no good for him to be set apart for the good of his fellow men if he remains cut off from them; and though his priesthood is primarily for others, it will not be entirely fruitful unless the others are able to get to him. It will lose much of its true meaning. It is not a denial of the world, nor a rejection of it, that leads the priest to give up even the legitimate pleasures of human life; it is rather for the sake of the world that he does it. The priest's vow of celibacy is a difficult thing. It means more than giving up the pleasures of the flesh; it means giving up the far more subtle joys of married life: the pleasant companionship of another; the continued, daily interest of another in one's work; the safety of a home and children — *his* children — where a man can retreat from the world and regroup his forces; the constant love of a faithful partner as life draws to an end. At first glance it would seem that a priest embraces a hideously lonely life; and it would be if it were not for this greater concern for the many. He gives up, at no little cost, the joys of a personal family, only that he might open his heart to all mankind. His celibacy does not make him *less* social; rather, it makes his life *more* social-minded, for he assumes that way of life for the sake of others.

In the same way, the priest is obliged to give up other concerns of life. His worldly possessions must not stand between him and his flock; nor his own will. He is a priest at all times, at all hours. He must set aside his own preferences for the good of others, for they all have rights over him. It is for this also that the priest needs deep sanctity, for without it he will not be accessible. To sacrifice oneself to others is not always an easy task; human weakness will rebel at it, and divine strength alone will make it possible. It is this alone that will enable him to adapt himself at once, sharing first the joys and then the sorrows of his flock; giving a sympathetic ear to all who seek his help; putting his own personal cares aside, and devoting all his energy to the problems of his fellow men.

The faithful have always sensed the presence of Christ in their priests. Even those men and women who would never stop to think that Christ lives in all His members, have had no trouble seeing in the priest "another Christ." That is the basic explanation for the respect given to the priest by the Catholic people. Christ Himself is really the *only* Priest; all others, bishops and priests alike, only share in the priesthood of Christ. They are but instruments of the great High Priest; they will all, bishop and priest alike, devote their lives to making the concern of Christ for His flock something very personal, very intimate. Until the end of time, then, Christ will supply the spiritual needs of His members. Through His priests, Christ will lift up the tiny infant to pour the redeeming waters of baptism upon his head. Through them, Christ the Priest will turn to the repentant sinner with words of comfort and the peace of forgiveness; through them, He will accompany His members throughout their lives; He will nourish their souls with His life-giving Body and Blood; He will witness their nuptials, as at Cana; He will come to visit the sick and keep watch at the bedside of the dying; He will stand at the open grave and commend their souls to His heavenly Father. He will speak words of comfort and of love; He will instruct; He will, if need be, reprove. But He does all things as a loving Father, and it is because His members see the Great High Priest in His ordained ministers, and see His love in what they do, that they address them by the exalted title of "Father" as well.

CHAPTER IX

THE TEACHER

*We know that thou hast come
a teacher from God. . . .*

ONE of the chief tasks assumed by Christ, apart from His priestly office, was that of teaching mankind eternal truth. He came to this earth to complete the divine revelation which alone gives the proper answer to the meaning of life. "God, who at sundry times and in divers manners spoke in times past to the fathers by the prophets, last of all in these days has spoken to us by his Son. . . ." This work of Christ must also continue in His members. Through them, Christ must continue to interpret life from *His* point of view: the *Christian* point of view. He will do that, of course, through the preaching of His priests and bishops, but He must continue this work on a far broader plain. Christ the Teacher must live on in schools; He must live on in the field of scholarship in general. "The first apostolate, at the present crossroads," writes Cardinal Suhard, "is in the realm of Thought. Need we add that this task is incumbent on the intellectuals, as it was in the time of the great Doctors of the Church? They must bend every possible effort to the creation of a Christian society in which the kingdom of God will be sought above all else."

The network of Catholic schools throughout the world is striking evidence of how Christ the Teacher lives on in His Church. It begins early enough in life, on the primary level. Thousands upon thousands of religious Brothers and Sisters and priests devote their lives to training the minds of the young. Their work in the classroom is something more than merely "teaching." It is an *apostolate. They are* Christ, forming in His youngest members a Christian mentality. The grade school level is not the very beginning of that training; it must have had its real start in the home. But when a child leaves the sanctuary of the home, and enters upon his formal education, he must not lose the spirit of Christ. The school is, in a way, a continuation of the home; for a child who comes from a Christian home, "school" means a Christian school. Even though the young boy or girl is learning nothing more than the alphabet or the way to add and subtract, his learning must carry with it the imprint of Christ's message. Religion can never be adequately tacked on, patchwork fashion, to an education received according to another system of thought; the sanguine hope that it might represents little more than wishful thinking.

"Education" is one of those words that we use daily but seldom define. It is, in reality, a word with a very broad meaning. A man is not educated if he merely knows how to read and write, and has stored away a fairly respectable number of "facts." He is not learned if he has simply mastered one or another technique: how to plow a field or run a machine or supervise a bus depot. An educated man is a man who has grasped a unified view of life. He is better able to acquire such a view, no doubt, if he has more *means* at his disposal: the ability to read, and the like. But a formal education alone will never assure us that a man is educated; a man with *no* "schooling" can still be a very "educated" man.

For a Christian, this unified view of life must include at all stages those truths given to man by God Himself. It means that Christ must go on teaching through His members because apart from Him and His revelation, human life will remain forever a hopeless enigma. To attempt to train a child in the various arts and sciences without viewing them in the light of Christ will result only in a warped perspective. Here in the United States the members of Christ's Mystical Body have assumed tremendous burdens to insure a truly *Christian* education for their children. They are not really against the system of public schools; as far as they go, these schools are excellent. But the goal of public education in America does not go far enough; it excludes God. Originally this was not the intention of those Americans who founded our country, but with the passing of time, other voices were raised to exclude Christian truth more and more. And today, those voices veritably shout their words under cover of "separation of Church and State." Religion, they say, must be excluded from our schools as a "working principle." It will help us to get along better. Yet whether God and Christian truth be excluded as a working principle or because of hearty disbelief, the final result is the *same:* a godless education. And that is what they want. Separation of Church and State will really mean separation of *God* and State.

Religion, however, is not a *part* of life; it is *all* of life. If the coming of Christ affects everything we do, we cannot afford to ignore Him in our schools. If we do, our way of life will become more and more a godless way of life. We will live according to that view of life by which we have been trained, that is, a philosophy of disbelief. A child who *hears* nothing about God will live about the same as the child who is taught that there *is* no God; or if the child hears about God only on Sundays, with no mention of Him during the week, he cannot help but look upon God as someone rather unimportant, perhaps unreal.

The young Sister, then, who spends long hours in the first grade classroom is really doing the work of Christ; she *is* Christ, teaching this particular little part of the world the meaning of life according to His point of view. She is not simply a woman who happens to be teaching; far more, she is doing the work of Christ. Christ the Teacher lives on in the thousands of Brothers and Sisters and priests and laymen and women who fill our classrooms. It is a dignity of which they must all be conscious. They do not simply have a "job"; they are engaged in an apostolate. This is carried on beyond the grade school, to the high school, the college, the university; and it is most important to remember that with each advance in learning a man should make progress in Christian insight as well. If he does not, what we have come to describe as "Catholic education" loses the very reason for its existence. It might even, in a certain sense, become dangerous, for as Pius XII pointed out to a group of young people: "You must flee from tiny manuals, which are insufficient for men of culture, and guard yourselves against a superficiality which creates easy illusions, and then unfailingly brings delusions to him who is satisfied with memorized formulas. The ever growing development of your historical, literary, and scientific knowledge, without the necessary adequate deepening of religion, could be most dangerous to your souls."

The purpose of the Church will not be achieved, however, if we go no further. It is not enough to set up a complete system of "our" schools, where we train our youth to live in what remains a fairly pagan world. Christ came as a challenge to the world; He will not be satisfied with a "ghetto" system — a closed world, as it were. We need Catholic schools to preserve and promote Christian learning, but not to isolate it there. Those who possess the truth of Christ must go forth in His name and bring that truth to others; they must make an impact upon the modern world of thought. That Harvard and Yale and the state universities have become the leaders of thought in America, indicates at least a partial failure on the part of Catholics. If institutions whose names are almost synonymous with "secularism" hold the first place, it means that something is wrong. Christianity once held that place; Christian truth — theology — was not excluded from the university campus.

Christ the Teacher, then, must also go out to meet mankind today on the field of scholarship. The men and women of His Church who hold teaching positions in the public schools or the universities must do what they can to make Christ heard. There are thousands of men and women, first of all, who conduct classes in our public school system. According to the accepted policies of those schools, these teachers cannot speak openly concerning their particular religious beliefs. Their apostolate in that regard is admittedly limited; and considering the circumstances and the situation, we might not wish it to be different. Until religious instruction is officially admitted into our school system, no Catholic would want to attempt to "indoctrinate" his students by subtle or underhanded means. But he should take the place of Christ and work to promote these general basic

Christian truths which played so large a part in the thinking of our founding fathers.

He must also watch to see that this "neutrality" is kept as conscientiously by others; he can see to it that others do not "indoctrinate" their *own* religious or, rather, "irreligious" views. These latter form the greater problem. An English teacher, for example, can do much in this regard by a series of subtle remarks about the "superstition of God" or the "outmoded standards of the Commandments." And he can get away with it only too often. His discussion of a poem can become the occasion for speaking about the "slavery of Romanism." An essay can bring up the question of the "unscientific views in religious belief." Literature has never accomplished what our American school system is at present attempting; it has never succeeded in cutting itself off completely from Christian philosophy or theology. Such questions arise constantly. When they do, Christ the Teacher would seek, through His members, the fairness, at least, that is officially a part of the system.

On a higher level, there is no reason why the apostolate of the Christian scholar should be so limited at all. The enemies of religion have a two-edged sword that they use to great advantage. A man may enter his university classroom and teach atheism, communism, immoral standards of conduct and then defend his action as "academic freedom." If, however, the man in the next classroom speaks of God or Christianity or the standards of the Ten Commandments, he is at once condemned. The flag of "academic freedom" is quickly run down, and that of "separation of Church and State" takes its place. What it amounts to is this: a man is free to teach anything that his view of life includes, *provided* it includes nothing in favor of God, religion, or Christian morality. So long as such a situation continues, Christianity cannot help but lose on the battlefield of the intellectuals. The believer will have nothing more to do than run back to his "own" university, and say what he has to say to those who already agree with him. He can only hope that they in turn will go out and succeed better than he in making some dent upon the rest of the world of thought.

Like Paul at Athens, the Christian teacher must seek an opportunity to be heard at the Areopagus. He must have discussions "in the market place every day with those who are there." He need not apologize for his message; he must speak it with conviction. He must speak it in those places where it is most needed. A Catholic who teaches at a state university is not just a teacher who happens to be a Catholic. He is Christ in that university; he must do what he can to speak in the name of Christ. There is no earthly reason why every form of nonsense should echo across the campuses of the world, while the mention of Christian truth should be forbidden. Christ must not be silenced.

A prerequisite for the privilege of speaking is the acquiring of true scholarship. We have need of *Catholic scholars.* A man's Catholicism cannot take the place of his scholarship, any more than mere scholarship could make up for the lack of Catholicism. They must be scholars who are accepted not because they are Catholic, but simply because they are scholars. This takes work and time; it means entire devotion to one's field. Our learned men must be able to stand side by side with *any* man in their field, and be accepted as his intellectual equal.

But something more. When a man scales these heights, he must not leave his faith behind him. His particular task — one that can be performed by no one else — is to integrate Christian truth into his field of specialization. He seeks only the truth; he will not let his religious views prejudice his scientific conclusions. But at the end, he will hold it up to the light of Christianity, in order to have a total view of things as they *really are.* No matter what the field, this must be true: literature, physics, biology, social science, labor relations, governmental theory. It is most often only through Christians in those fields that other men will hear the message of Christ and see His viewpoint. These others may never come in contact with a priest, but they will associate daily with these members of Christ who are their fellow teachers and friends. In the circumstances of our modern world, it often happens that unless Christ speaks through those fellow teachers, He speaks not at all. They have as much right as any other to take part in seeking the truth, to engage in all controversies, to add their solution. As other

Christs, they have an obligation to do so. Their faith is not something to be hidden under a bushel, but to be shared with all mankind. To them also did Christ say: "You are the light of the world."

The work of the scholar is sometimes looked upon as a rather humorous affair, hopelessly impractical. We find out too late, however, that we were wrong. Men spend one generation trying to correct the evils they laughed at a hundred years before. Many men thought that the philosophy of Hegel was certainly sheer nonsense when he first produced it, but when we see it today, put into practice in world-wide Communism, we see our error. As Bishop Sheen once wrote: "When society finds it is too late to electrocute a thought, it electrocutes the man." A far better place to start is in the field of thought. It is a place that offers far greater hope of success as well.

Christian teachers and scholars need never apologize for their work. It is of first-rank importance. Christ needs to continue enlightening the world; they must be the means of His doing that. With his customary insight, Cardinal Suhard summed up their task in these words. "Your task, Christian thinkers, is not to follow, but to lead. It is not enough to be disciples, you must become masters; it is not enough to imitate, you must invent. . . . You will not hesitate to give yourselves entirely and in the joy of knowing to your vocation of scholars. . . . You will not hesitate, either, to apply your researches to the field of civilization. For the problem is to build a new world, to define and prepare the structures which will permit man to be fully man, in a City worthy of him, to transfigure all things in order to make of them a Christian world."

CHAPTER X

THE CHRISTIAN IN BUSINESS

---

*Thou shalt love thy
neighbor as thyself. . . .*

IN OUR workaday world, there are thousands of men and women who have a special opportunity to demonstrate the fervor of Christian love. They have chosen as their life's work one or another of those tasks which bring them into daily contact with their neighbor. It is a real tragedy when they come to look upon what they do as nothing more than a "job." There are those men and women who help in the formation of the home: maids, housekeepers; or those people who come in contact with the needs of the home: the butchers, the grocers, salesmen, milkmen; the jeweler, the telephone operator, the repairman, the mailman, the tailor, and a host of others. No man lives alone, segregated from other men. We can easily note the dependence of society on the workingman. What he does in his factory or in his office will serve the needs of countless thousands of his fellow men. In his case, however, they are countless thousands whom he will most likely never see; there is something impersonal about his daily work — and it is this that makes it doubly hard. Part of ennobling the worker's vocation lies in bringing about a clearer grasp of this social element. Only if this is done can he come to think of himself as a human being, helping society, instead of a machine turning out products. In a way, the "labor problem" is a problem of human relations; it can be solved only by those who understand what human nature is.

On the other hand, it might seem, at first glance, that workers who find themselves in daily contact with people would see the social element in their lives more easily. The strange fact is that often they do not. What our modern society has lost almost completely, and on so many levels, is a well-developed *social sense.*

Those men who deal with people have a special opportunity to give a living example of how Christ would deal with them. Insofar as they are businessmen, they will naturally strive to be honest and dependable. Insofar as they are workers, they will be just; they will do what is expected of them. But above all, since they are in such close contact with other people, they will also show forth the spirit of Christian love. They will be Christ, serving others, helping them, doing good to them. A restaurant will be a "Christian" restaurant only if the spirit of Christ dwells there; it will be that, only if the owner is good and honest, and the workers sincere and dependable. But above all, it will be "Christian" only if all are imbued with real Christian love. A copy of Dale Carnegie in every waiter's pocket may help to win friends and influence people, but the spirit of Christ will go much further than that. The motto of Benedictine hospitality is to "treat every guest as another Christ." That has meaning. Christ has got to live throughout society; He must capture it entirely, and that means in our stores, our restaurants, on our delivery trucks, our milk routes, in the hearts of all.

As we have said before, the need to re-emphasize the social side of human life is being met by two distinct doctrines: the doctrine of Communism and the doctrine of the Mystical Body. The Christian world is turning more and more to St. Paul's manner of speech, and is learning to think of the Church in terms of the Body of Christ. It is here that we find the human unity that God intended as the crown of man's social striving. Communism would unite mankind by destroying the worth of the individual; Christianity would unite mankind by elevating the worth of the individual to the level of Christ. It is in Christ and through Christ that all men would find the noblest bond of union. Communism would erase distinctions by making the individual man nothing; Christianity would blot out distinctions by making every man Christ.

This twofold secret of Christianity can come to play an important role in the lives of these men and women who must deal with their fellow men: to see Christ in themselves, and to see Christ in others. "Christ is all things and in all." The spirit of His love then will show forth in what they say and what they do. St. Paul's is still the best description of what Christian love will look like:

> Charity is patient, is kind;
>   charity does not envy, is not pretentious,
> is not puffed up, is not ambitious,
>   is not self-seeking, is not provoked;
> thinks no evil, does not rejoice over wickedness,
>   but rejoices with the truth;
> bears all things, believes all things,
> hopes all things, endures all things.

All of this can help to brighten the life of the Christian in his associations with other people. Surely the harassed clerk in a department store can understand the need for patience. It is not enough for a Christian to "endure" a customer or to put on a false front; his love must come from the heart, and show itself in patience and kindness. Kindness is something that means so much; we can find it in a smile, a friendly greeting. To live in that spirit continually, however, we need the love of Christ dwelling in our heart; it means overcoming our own ill will and ugliness. The members of Christ must show this spirit; they need to be something more than just "honest" business people; they need to be other Christs.

Many of these vocations demand a great amount of concern for one's fellow men, a real devotion to the common good. It must be the members of Christ who are engaged in those tasks who will work to transform that devotion and that concern into Christian love. We know the risks involved in the life of a fireman, for example, or a policeman; we are all moved by the story of a telephone operator who gave her life in a flood by remaining at her post to help others; we marvel at the heroism of the forest patrol who risk their lives to save families trapped in a forest fire. There are many jobs that demand that a person dedicate his life to the service of others, even to the extent of giving up his life in their behalf. Certainly there is a way to supernaturalize these highest of natural sentiments, to make them reflect the image of Christ.

Some of these men and women will help complete the work of the home. The family is as a rule no longer self-sufficient; we need others who will help supply our needs of food and clothing. Viewed in this light, their work is not simply a means of making money. There is something truly social about it; what they do touches upon the lives of others. It helps to realize that. A grocery man is not merely selling vegetables; he is helping to provide for the needs of a hundred different families. If he approaches his job in that spirit, he will not want to cheat his customers, because he will see his Christian obligation toward them. Men must work together in order to strengthen the social bonds between them, and we must do that even between our home and the corner store. There are many opportunities to exercise charity toward the needy in such a case. A businessman might frown upon such practices; a Christian would not, even though he knows he will receive nothing in return. "If you lend to those from whom you hope to receive in return, what merit have you? For even sinners lend to sinners that they may get back as much in return. But love your enemies; and do good, and lend, not hoping for any return, and your reward shall be great. . . ." Christ would act in that fashion; He asks His members to do the same.

People in our modern society also find themselves dependent upon their fellow men for houses in which to live. We need Christian landlords today: men who will not raise their rents so high that the ordinary family cannot afford to live in a decent place; men who will not hang such abominable and un-Christian signs as "No children allowed" or "No more than two children permitted." They must act as Christ would in their place. If they feel that human prudence would dictate otherwise, let them follow the "foolishness of God," for it is "wiser than men."

Some people will find that they must in a way take the place of the home. For a Christian, a boardinghouse should not be just a house; it should be a home. A hotel must not be something completely divorced from the spirit of Christ; it should not be, as it so often is, a place where men close one eye to wickedness, and make sin easy. Christian love does not "rejoice over wickedness," nor dismiss it with a shrug. There is nothing that should not come under the rule of Christ, no place where Christian love would not fit in.

Today the tavern and the cocktail lounge have become a common meeting place, but hardly a place for Christianity. And yet, why not? They are not bad in themselves, and if they are going to have a place in life, they can be Christian. A member of Christ who works in a tavern cannot feel that he is living as Christ would have him, as long as he continues to take the weekly wage of a man and turn him out, staggering into the night. He can't answer that "If I don't take it, someone else will; business is business." There is such a thing as integrity. A Christian would rather not prosper, if his prosperity means the ruin of another man's life.

Such things are not outlandish or fanatical. There have been taverns where Catholics have carried on a real apostolate. One place, for example, is run by a very devout couple, well rooted in their faith. They manage to preserve a Christian spirit without becoming preachy. They steadfastly refuse to sell any liquor to those who have already had enough; they will never sell to one who is too young. They have a piano off in one corner, away from the bar, and they encourage their customers to gather there, and play and sing together. They purposely try to foster a family spirit, but they allow no drunkenness or rowdiness. Very much of life passes before them. Their friends return to seek their advice, and much sound advice is given. As the wife cooks the steaks in which they specialize, she wants to know whom they are for, because she looks upon all her patrons as members of her family. They could enlarge, and double their business, but they will not; they are doing well enough, and they feel that they are also accomplishing a certain purpose in life by helping those about them.

There is an endless list of possibilities for bringing Christ into His rightful place in society. It is a rather foolish notion that to be a good follower of Christ you must live in a monastery; but it is even more foolish for a man to think that if he does not live in a monastery, he need not live as a Christian except on Sunday mornings. That type of man is the very one who would feel that Christ was out of place except in the temple. There were men like that at the time of Christ also, men who would have Him stay hidden away. When our Lord chose Matthew as one of His disciples, some were scandalized. Levi, as Matthew was also called, was a tax-collector. His friends and associates were not always the best type of individuals from the world's point of view. As St. Luke tells us: "Levi gave a great feast for him at his house; and there was a great gathering of publicans and of others, who were at the table with them." The Pharisees and their Scribes thought Christ was out of place. "Why do you eat and drink with publicans and sinners?" they asked. "And Jesus answered and said to them, 'It is not the healthy who need a physician, but they who are sick. I have not come to call the just, but sinners to repentance.'"

Christ, then, must speak. He must speak about the need of a just wage for the laborer. He must speak of a fair return for the investments of capital, while seeking also a fair distribution of the profits of industry on the side of the laborer. He must speak of "social justice," even when men tell Him to say no more than the Lord's Prayer. He must speak out against the abuses of power on the side of labor unions as well as on the side of capital. He must seek to promote honesty and integrity on all sides.

The worker does not always respect this honesty, and insofar as he fails, he reflects less the spirit of Christ. He may make unjust claims, he may seek an unfair advantage. He may refuse to give an honest day's labor for what he has agreed to accept in payment. And the owner or employer, on the other hand, may violate Christian honesty just as badly. He may refuse a just wage, or he may cheat his creditors. He may try to divide his moral life from his business life with the foolish statement that "business is business; let's keep religion out of this." He may fail in his Christian attitude by regarding his workers as no more than machines, feeling that once he has paid for them all his obligations cease. Whether they are single or married, or whether they have many children or none, will be none of his concern. His "machines" all cost the same price.

Rooting out these false attitudes is no easy task. The worker and the employer play the essential role in the process, but many others must also take part. The scholar and the teacher must delve into these subtle problems, and pass them on to their students. Leaders of our governments must turn their attention in that direction, and the citizens in general must, through study and discussion, become increasingly aware of what the problem involves. But above all, Christ must live in the parties most concerned — the men who labor in the stores and factories and offices, and the men who own those businesses. They must come to look upon one another as *brothers in Christ, as partners,* engaged in a common task. They must provide for the mutual interests of both sides, harming neither one nor the other.

Christ must live in the store, the office; He must live in the man who runs a tailor shop or a restaurant. We cannot imagine Christ the Carpenter cheating the patrons of His shop at Nazareth nor overcharging them nor giving them a cheap imitation of what they thought they were getting. "Business is business" sounds every bit as shocking coming from the members of Christ as it would have sounded coming from His own lips.

This is the spirit of the Christian: to bring Christ to those places, to those problems which need Him. Modern man is sick, and Christ alone can cure Him. And it is the love of Christ's members that must bring the two together. The Christian will not quit the world, and leave what remains to the power of Satan. The Christian must seek out the world. "The modern apostolate can in no wise adopt a negative attitude of retreat or of protection from pernicious influences, nor just a propaganda, nor even a 'conquest,' if we understand by this an exterior annexation of subjects or human currents. The victory of the Church," warns Cardinal Suhard, "is not a matter of isolation. . . . The Christian's effort will not consist only in recruiting, and of making unbelievers 'come to him,' but especially of mixing with them to save them as they are: a centrifugal action which must make of the Church the 'leaven' of the immense mass, and the young blood which will give it life."

CHAPTER XI

THE WRITER

What I tell you in darkness,
speak it in the light;
and what you hear whispered,
preach it on the housetops. . . .

THE Christian is a man with a message, the message of Christ. As a member of the Mystical Christ, he must continue to repeat that message in all the corners of the earth, until the end of time. He must make use of every means at his disposal to implant this truth in the hearts of men. This was one of the basic principles in the apostolic thought of Pius XI. "It is urgently necessary," he wrote, "to make provisions that whatever of God's gifts the progress of the age may have added either to human learning or to technical and scientific skill, shall in this field also be ordained to His glory and to the salvation of souls, and shall be made to promote in a practical way the extension of the kingdom of God upon earth."

It is because of this that we find the Christian turning his attention to the fields of literature and the arts; it is on this account that he has an interest in the field of entertainment. These are the powerful means of influencing the mass of humanity, and the forces of good must make use of them no less than the forces of evil.

The mightiest of these aids has been traditionally found in the pen. The writer finds himself in a most unique position for influencing the minds of others. What he writes may be read and reread at leisure, and passed on to others. In the past, when life presented fewer distractions, men possibly read more than they do today. At present, a man need not be a cynic to suspect that a fairly small percentage of the books that are bought actually manage to get read; our book-club age is frequently satisfied with saying "I must buy that book," instead of "I must read it." Regardless, the writer today still holds a unique position, perhaps one of even greater importance than in the past, because those men who actually *do* read will be among the most influential. They will be the men who, in turn, control the minds of many another; they are the men who are not afraid to think. Subversive elements among us realize this, and they write without ceasing; they seek every opportunity to infiltrate their thought into the minds of men. Those who would fashion the "mind of Christ" must do as much and more. And they share that responsibility with those who especially will bring the books to the readers: with the booksellers, librarians, book reviewers.

The most obvious requirement of anything we might term Christian literature is twofold: it must be truly Christian, and it must be literature. When we look over the field, we might find confusion on both points. There is some very subtle and elusive quality that marks off a piece of literature from run-of-the-mill writing. It is the result of talent and training, of good taste and style, of hard work and genius. But it does no good to lower our standards when dealing with a writer who happens to be a Catholic. If the members of Christ are to assume an important place in the world of literature, what they produce must be real literature. We gain nothing by trying to push a second-rate poet into a first-rate class simply because he is a Christian, or because he writes about religious topics. Occasionally we find a writer who does not expend the time and energy needed to perfect his writing talent, but who feels that his Christianity should make up the difference. He accuses those "of the world" who criticize his work of being prejudiced against his faith, when such is really not the case.

From the apostolic point of view, it is important that the member of Christ produce real literature because only then will those outside the fold read what he writes. In the same way, a man who aims at producing a scientific work instead of literature must be sure that his scholarship is solid, his method truly scientific, and his style clear and appealing. Otherwise he will not command respect in those very circles where he should be read. There is a very real danger here of creating a specifically "Catholic" reading public. They will put up with a lot of badly written books because they are about Catholic people or Catholic topics. They will not be too critical of a rather unscientific presentation, filled with pious platitudes, because they are in hearty agreement with the writer before they begin to read. Part of raising the level of writing in Catholic life lies in raising the standards of the Catholic reading public, training them to demand the best.

The heart of the question lies in just what the term "Christian literature" means. If the members of Christ must bring something special to this field, just what is it? It certainly is not Christian "propaganda" — making use of the written word by obviously forcing Christian truths into contexts where they do not fit. There must be some sort of blending, or we destroy what should be literature. Much of what passes for Catholic literature falls into this class unfortunately. We run across a short story that is patently aimed at showing the evil of birth control, or a novel that tells about the happiness of cloistered nuns, wrapping that message about a very weak and flimsy story. The result is not always too appealing.

Quite often we rally about something we acclaim as Christian literature simply because the author is a Christian, or because he writes about a priest or a nun or a family that goes to Church. Surely the connection between the writing and Christianity should be something more profound. The theme should in some way flow from our Christianity. If we could remove all the references to religion and religious truth, and leave the story intact, our Christianity would be no more than trimming. Such a condition would hardly help people to grasp the essential importance of these truths in life.

Nor would a story that depends upon the miraculous ever reach the heart of a Christian way of life through that alone. Miracles and visions have great popular appeal, and they are a part of Christianity, but they are something out of the ordinary. Our Christian faith does not stand or fall, dependent upon any particular event of that kind.

A zealous preacher once related how a certain man could not bring himself to accept the definition of Pius IX in 1854 concerning the Immaculate Conception of the Blessed Virgin. When Mary herself appeared at Lourdes a few years later, however, and told Bernadette that "I am the Immaculate Conception," the man's difficulties supposedly vanished. Actually, for one with a proper understanding of his faith, the definitive words of the Pope would have settled the issue, and would always have had greater meaning than the account of a private vision. Surely if the Blessed Mother had never appeared at Lourdes, the belief of the Church in her Immaculate Conception would not have been lessened at all.

In our search for some key to the direction in which the Christian writer must go, we are led back to the basic notions. Imaginative literature aims at presenting an *interpretation* of life; it deals with general themes, treating man as he *really is*. It is here that Christian reality enters the picture. Man as he really is, lives in a supernatural order. He is a creature wounded by sin, redeemed by Christ, and destined to gain eternal happiness by joining himself, here upon earth, to the life and the mission of Christ. Christian literature views human life in that light; it places human life in its proper background. Sin marks a failure in our love of God; virtue means the triumph of His grace. Christian literature is not content with telling what a man does; it goes on to point out the hand of God in what we see. It attaches itself to that cosmic view of St. Paul when he cried out: "For me, to live is Christ."

The vocation of the Christian journalist must follow the same lines. He must be another Christ, interpreting life in the light of Christ's teaching. He must, of course, be a good journalist, but he must be something more. The genius of Catholic journalism will lie particularly in its ability to *interpret* events in a totally Christian way. It may be a secondary purpose of a Catholic newspaper to record events of importance in the diocese or the world; and a Catholic magazine may try to give light reading for the leisure hours. But the special gift of the Catholic journalist lies in what he can do that is different from others. The recording of parish card parties will not necessarily make a Catholic newspaper, any more than stories about nuns will make a

Catholic magazine. We cannot be satisfied with producing "secular magazines," written and edited by Catholics.

With our magazines, we run the same risk that we encounter with books: the danger of creating an exclusively Catholic reading public. Catholic books about Catholic subjects written by Catholic writers for Catholic readers; thus do we set the stage of a "ghetto" Christianity. The vocation of the members of Christ in the field of journalism must also be apostolic. They need to break into the magazines that are read far and wide, in all circles. Only in that way can they bring the influence of Christ into the entire field, and make His presence felt where it is most needed.

Being an apostle is not the same, of course, as being a propagandist. Some people have a difficult time telling the difference. The word "propaganda" seems to imply some notion of a trick or a scheme. We think of a man slyly wedging his ideas into every empty space; we think of someone who colors the truth a bit to make his case more potent; we think of a man repeating his ideas so often and so forcefully that he literally beats us into accepting them. "If you repeat a lie often enough, people will soon begin to think it is the truth." The apostle will have none of that. He deals only with the truth, and his greatest weapon is the truth: the allurement that truth itself has for the human mind. But the apostle, like the propagandist, knows that he must get his ideas before the minds of those men whom he would win. If he cannot do that, his apostolate becomes stagnant.

The need for good, apostolic "Catholic" magazines and books is great at present because we must, unfortunately, retrain the Catholic populace. They are, by and large, a rather unapostolic group, only too ready to push the responsibility of refashioning a new world on to the shoulders of the priests and religious. They need to become conscious of their dignity as members of Christ's Mystical Body, and their vocation as apostles. But such books and magazines do not constitute our final goal. The writer must still, once he has realized his vocation, reach out toward the mass of men who are awaiting in darkness the vision of Christ.

The danger in both these cases is the danger of "watering down" Catholic doctrine. Our present "Catholic" magazines might tend to oversimplify. Following the trend of much modern journalism, they hesitate to ask their readers to think; and when they do that, they defeat their very purpose. The emphasis upon mass circulation by some publications results in a type of popularization that reduces many statements to the point where they fail to have the desired good effect upon the readers. We cannot form apostles by making truths meaningless. One of the greatest challenges thrust upon the Catholic writer is the need to discuss things that cannot be made overly simple. He must ask his readers to come up to a higher level. His solutions cannot be pictured in a comic book. If the Catholic press aims at a low common denominator of mental and spiritual development, we can never hope for an *apostolic* laity. And we should not look down upon the intellectual ability of most men; they are often capable of far more than current opinion will credit them. "Never underestimate the intelligence of your audience," said Glenn Frank, "but never overestimate their information." If we lead them step by step, they will follow.

In trying to reach those outside the Church, we must also be careful not to betray our apostolate by watering down our statements in the hope of winning them over more easily. It is not a watered-down Christianity that holds the solution for the world's ills, and it is not the flimsy substitute for the real thing that will ultimately draw men to embrace the Christian way of life. The fullness of Christianity is what the world needs; a Christian faith that includes a visible church and a pope and visible sacraments as the means of grace and a corporate act of worship called the Mass. This is the Christianity that came from Christ, and that will save the world. We need not fear to offer the fullness of Christ's truth to the world; it is what the world needs. We may sound arrogant at first when we say that Christianity and Catholicism mean the same thing. Yet that is the truth, and it will not seem arrogant at all when it is recognized as the truth. What Christianity there is in the world apart from the Mystical Body of Christ is still derived from that Church. And it is to build up that visible Body, uniting all men in this social Body of Christ, that we labor. When we say *Christianity* we mean the *Catholic Church;* when we say the *Catholic Church,* we mean *Christ:* Christ living upon this earth in those who are His members.

CHAPTER XII

SOCIAL WORK

*By this will all men know
that you are my disciples,
if you have love for one another. . . .*

THE outstanding trait of Christianity has always been its spirit of love. "See how those Christians love one another!" cried pagan Rome. Christ brought a new meaning to the word "love." He raised it from a purely natural sentiment to something divine. He taught men to love as God loves: an unselfish love that empties itself for the good of others, but seeks no return. That is why Christ could say to His followers: "Love your enemies." Anyone can love those who are close to him, and who also love him; but it takes the love of Christ to reach out toward those who offer nothing in return. Society will always have large numbers who are in need of such Christian love. There will be men and women who must make demands upon the goodness of others, but who have little more than gratitude to return; there will be others who will not even have gratitude, but who need our love nonetheless.

As our modern world has gradually drawn away from Christ, we could easily suspect that its concern for the unfortunate would become less Christlike. But Christ must continue to preach His message in this modern world. We need His message, for in this era of world-wide "charity," we have lost "love." Our life today witnesses a constant procession of charitable appeals. We are forevermore adopting new "programs," building finer orphanages and homes, raising bigger funds, and envisioning greater "successes." But Christ is being pushed out of the picture more and more each day. Modern methods of organization have taken over, and possibly Christ looks rather "old fashioned" in our eyes. We feel that we have no personal responsibility toward the needy; all we need is the address and the phone number of the nearest agency. We contribute toward their work, and they administer our "charity" for us. We seem to have forgotten that we cannot organize love, nor meet the needs of the human heart by filling out application blanks and compiling statistics.

Christ would feel hopelessly out of place in a good many of our present-day social agencies, even some that claim to be Christian. He is *not* living in social work as He wants and as He must. His love would not be satisfied with the glassy stare of a paid worker, glaring over the counter. We cannot imagine Christ sitting behind a desk, cool and impersonal, without the slightest flicker of a smile, barking at the needy something like "What's *your* trouble?" We cannot think of Him embarrassing those in need by talking about their troubles in a loud voice at the front desk; we cannot think of Him making the unfortunate humiliate themselves before Him simply because they are in need. Christ, "meek and humble of heart," could show nothing but kindness under those circumstances. And Christian love must do the same.

The members of Christ who engage in social work can never be what the world calls "welfare workers." They must be something more; they must be other Christs. The special task of any Christian engaged in such work is to bring into that field the love of Christ. Any man can help develop more efficient means of administering charity, and more accurate ways of weeding out the undeserving. The techniques of social work can be perfected as we learn more and more about human nature. But we can never substitute techniques for Christian love. If the members of Christ who are doing this work are guilty of any great fault, it is undoubtedly their overawe at the progress of modern social methods. Surely we should make use of any means at our disposal to make our work more efficient, but when we become efficient at the cost of Christian love, we lose our special gift. If these members of Christ keep always His spirit of love, they need never feel abashed or inferior in the face of any larger, more modern, more organized social agency. They have the one thing that no other men can have, and that no system can replace, no matter how highly developed it may be. They have the love of Christ.

As other Christs, then, they must not feel that they should become more and more like the typical "modern" agency. Rather, they should feel that the modern agency should become more and more like them; they should feel that it also should breathe the spirit of Christian love. Modern methods offer much to improve the work of Christian social agencies; what they contribute, however, is as nothing in comparison to what the Christian can give to modern charity. We tend so much to depersonalize our charity today; we tend to shift the entire responsibility to the State, with its massive system of organization and its necessarily impersonal manner. We need to return to the way of Christ. We must even get back to that spirit where one man will help his next-door neighbor directly instead of offering to drive him to the nearby agency — even if it is a Catholic agency. The charity of Christ must find a place in the heart of *every* member of Christ. It is only emphasized by those who choose it as their lifework, or who devote a large part of their spare time to charity; by no means do they have a monopoly upon such love. It is rather frightening to hear that the family of a sick woman must go untended because she cannot afford to hire help, and because her Christian neighbors next door are too busy watching television or playing cards to lend a helping hand. "Why don't they call the county?" they ask. Would Christ have ever uttered such a question?

We need such personal, neighborly charity, even in the matter of extending financial help. When a man can afford to help another, he certainly acts in a more Christian way if he does so, instead of referring the needy man to the State. The Christian, like Christ, must be ever restless about the needs of others. There is something very shocking about two brothers arguing in the courts over thousands of dollars, while the family of a third brother has no house to live in; but it happens even among those who claim to be Christian. But even beyond the boundaries of our immediate family, there are others who may need the assistance we are well able to give. Christian love will not pass them by.

There is also something very special about Christian charity that is sometimes forgotten. It lies in this, that it seeks no return. How many times we hear people relate how much they have done for another, and complain that they "never get a thing back from him!" How often our modern social agencies resemble loan offices instead of charitable organizations. The distinguishing feature of Christian charity is that it seeks no return; its value lies in the *giving*. Even if the one who receives is ungrateful or wastes our gifts or accepts them under false pretenses, he cannot deprive our giving of its value as an act of Christian love; its value springs from the spirit within our own heart.

Christ summed up His entire philosophy of charity in that beautiful passage from the Gospel of St. Luke that leaves the non-Christian so bewildered:

> But I say to you who are listening: Love your enemies,
>   do good to those who hate you,
> Bless those who curse you, pray for those who calumniate you.
> And to him who strikes thee on the one cheek, offer the other also;
>   and from him who takes away thy cloak, do not withhold thy tunic.
> Give to everyone who asks of thee,
>   and from him who takes away thy goods, ask no return.
> And even as you wish men to do to you, so also do you to them.
> And if you love those who love you, what merit have you?
>   For even sinners do that.
> And if you lend to those from whom you hope to receive in return,
>   what merit have you?
>   For even sinners lend to sinners that they may get back as much in
>   return.
> But love your enemies; and do good, and lend, not hoping for any
>   return, and your reward shall be great,
>   and you shall be children of the Most High,
>   for he is kind towards the ungrateful and evil.
> Be merciful, therefore, even as your Father is merciful.

There are three different types of people who will especially need our help: those who are in temporal need because of their own mistakes, those in want because of another, and those in spiritual poverty.

There are in society a certain number of people who have never managed to adjust themselves to the demands of adult life. They are the people who can never hold a job; they are the men and women who become alcoholics and drug addicts and moral degenerates because of their immaturity. It is from this group also that there come most often the "fakers," who try to make a living by appeals to charity. As a rule, these people do not lack opportunity as much as they lack the ability to achieve maturity. They are really sick, and more than anything else they need medical and psychiatric treatment that may help them to grow up. It is good to know, of course, what they need. Yet, despite that deeper psychological need, they also are tired and hungry and homeless from time to time; because of that, they too have a claim on our temporal gifts, even though it may seem that their own foolishness and perversity have brought them to that condition of need. They are, undoubtedly, the hardest to deal with, but for that very reason, Christian love is so much more necessary.

These people will often affect the lives of others. There are wives and children and aged parents who also are homeless and hungry because they cannot depend upon their husband or father or child. These must be helped, with real Christian charity. They are neither sick nor guilty; they are only in need. They are easier to deal with, provided we can put aside any resentment we might feel for the individual who has brought such suffering upon them. To say that the father or husband or son should take care of them is to state an obvious truth. But that will not fill their empty stomachs when he refuses.

The easiest of all to whom we might turn our charity are those who are in want simply because of misfortune — orphans and widows, the aged left entirely alone in the world, families in need because of war or flood or fire, men who have no work simply because there is no work to be found, try as they may. The human heart reaches out toward these quite naturally, and the obligation of charity has the added impulse of human emotion. But Christian love must reach to all of these people, even those of the very first group, who might arouse an opposite emotion of antagonism. The love of the Christian may be helped by human emotion, but it should not be hampered by it.

The last group of those who need our help are the sinners. This is a particularly Christian love, the love of the Good Shepherd. Sin lies rooted in the heart of every man, for in the sight of God we have all sinned. When we speak of those who need our special help, however, we don't mean ordinary sinners; we mean the real down-and-out sinners, who seem to be beyond reform. They have fallen so low that they can scarcely see the face of God. We must seek them out, and lift them up. The Good Shepherd must live on in His members.

This is difficult because sin when it reaches that level, is a very repulsive thing. At the beginning, sin may be rather attractive to some, but when it is an open, blatant affair, it loses even its apparent air of charm and allurement. It is no longer "clever" and "sophisticated." The Pharisees want nothing of it. It is here that the Christian sees more. Impressed upon every soul in baptism is the divine seal, the sacramental character of baptism; and because of that, even in the sinner, we can find the image of Christ. As Pius XII has told us: "Christ did not wish to exclude sinners from His Church; hence if some of her members are suffering from spiritual maladies, that is no reason why we should lessen our love for the Church, but rather a reason why we should increase our devotion to her members." When the Church sees these sick members, she does not abandon them; rather, "with the brave heart of a mother, she applies herself at once to the work of nursing them back to spiritual health." They are yet members of Christ. And even the unbaptized soul is destined for such glory. They are "our brothers in Christ according to the flesh, called, together with us, to the same eternal salvation."

Christ gave us an example in His kind regard for Magdalen and the Good Thief. We need that spirit to keep from making outcasts of any member of society. The Houses of the Good Shepherd throughout the world give a striking example of that Christian ideal. Yet, much as the average Catholic will approve of the work, would these same fallen women meet with that same love of Christ if he met them somewhere else? Do we — average Catholics — even show our Christian love within the ordinary happenings of our life? We might easily have taken part in the current gossip, and condemned the young unmarried girl who, because of one unfortunate failure, has become pregnant. She becomes the "talk of the town" among those who forget the many who have done the same thing with the protection of modern ingenuity. What is praised is not necessarily virtue but "smartness"; what is condemned is not necessarily vice but "stupidity." The Christian must see things in their true light.

Charity may never stop with bodily needs; it must go on and minister to souls, for it is there that the ultimate difficulties lie. That is the final lesson that Christ would teach those in social work, whether on a neighborly basis or an organized basis. The coldness, the impersonal quality of so much of our modern charity springs from the fact that it is a "soul-less" charity. If we limit ourselves to the externals, we may help to clothe bodies and feed hungry stomachs, but we may fail to help *people*. The social nature of man is rooted in his soul. If we forget his soul, he differs not at all from the animal; and if we look upon him in that light, it is not surprising if we begin to treat him as impersonally as we would a hungry dog.

To see Christ in ourselves; to see Christ in those we help; to give in the spirit of Christ, expecting no return. That is the spirit of the Christian social worker: to have Christ dwelling in his heart In this way only will the love of Christ reign supreme in the work of charity. In this way only will men know that we are the disciples of Christ, *other Christs,* aflame with love for one another.

CHAPTER XIII

THE CHRISTIAN WORKER

Is not this the carpenter,
the son of Mary . . . ?

CHRIST must have wanted to lay special emphasis upon the dignity of work because He spent so many years as a worker. He honored manual labor in a way that He honored nothing else, perhaps for good reason. The life of man upon this earth is a life of labor. The overwhelming majority of men will find themselves engaged in it. And when anything becomes very ordinary and usual, it is likely to lose its luster. Christ wanted to be sure that the worker would not miss the true meaning of what he does. Should a man complain and say that his hours of labor are nothing more than endless minutes of wasted time, Christ would turn and point to His own life. "Were those years nothing more than that?" It would seem quite ridiculous to say that the years spent by our Lord in the carpenter shop were wasted years; there could be nothing pointless in the life of Christ. It is just as ridiculous to say that of the members of Christ's Mystical Body. In all they do, Christ lives in them; they must have the spirit of Christ, they must "put on Christ." They must also be Christ: Christ the Worker.

There is a dignity and a sanctity to work that has been lost sight of in the modern world. Men have come to look upon it as a necessary evil rather than a means of serving God and neighbor. The difficulty

with such a view is obvious. If work is evil, and if it takes up so large
a portion of life, then life itself will seem to be evil. Life will lose its
meaning; it will lack direction and will be pointless. Yet St. Paul
would walk down the corridors of a factory today and say that "to
me to live is Christ." He would turn to the office worker and the
farmer, and repeat the same message. "You need not forget Christ
in what you do. Let Him fill your life, every minute of it. You are
doing now what Christ did for many long years; you are working.
Work then in the spirit of Christ, with the love of Christ, and with
His sense of dedication. Realize that what you do is not beneath your
dignity, if it was not beneath the dignity of the God-Man. You do not
degrade yourself by what you do. Raise up your head; you are other
Christs. You see, I also work. I am a tentmaker by trade, and like
you, I have toiled, working with my own hands."

Of all the segments of human life where the presence of Christ is
felt less and needed most, the portion belonging to the worker stands
out. "The great scandal of the nineteenth century," wrote Pius XI,
"was the loss of the working class to the Church." It is another way of
saying that the presence of Christ was not made real among those who
labor. As a result, their attitude toward work has not been the attitude
of Christ; the spirit, the atmosphere in which they live has been entirely
divorced from Christ. The world of the worker needs to return to this
twofold sense of dedication: the service of God and the love of neighbor. It is for God and neighbor that man will labor. Undoubtedly it is
easier for the individual to regain the notion of serving God in what
he does; the notion of serving our neighbor, however, seems strangely
foreign to our modern way of thinking. Our *social* conscience has only
recently been reawakened, and it is this that makes the problem so
difficult in general.

The tendency during the past centuries has been to look upon the
individual as all-important. Success was attributed to the talent of
the individual, and to no one else. We have built up the picture of
the self-made man who has made his own way in the world, using
men and machines in much the same fashion. We have lost our social
sense. There is, in point of fact, no self-made man. There is no man
upon earth who is not dependent upon other men in what he does,

no man who can achieve success without the help of others. The progress of society depends upon the co-operative effort of many men, and the tendency of some men to look down upon the "worker" means that they have forgotten how much they depend upon him. The great financier must have an office in which to work; his secretaries need typewriters and adding machines to keep his records; his wife needs furniture for the home, and he needs an automobile for travel. All of these are made by other men; without them, there would be no great financier. The same is true of every individual, no matter how much he may forget that fact. Society is one unit. Men need one another, they depend upon one another. The Christian, however, would ask not only that they admit it and act accordingly; he would ask also that they elevate their social nature to the level of Christ, where it will know its highest perfection.

This glorification of the self-made man has had its effect even among those who did not fit in that category. It has contributed immensely to the unrest of the worker. Only too often the worker is not interested in social problems *as such*. If he had the opportunity, he would be a "self-made man," according to the usual pattern — and a doubly selfish one at that. Lacking the opportunity, he is in perpetual turmoil; he cannot be satisfied with his lot. He cries out against abuses in the field of labor, but he does so, not because he thinks they indicate an abuse of the principles of justice. His cries are often motivated only by a cancerous envy; they give expression only to his feeling of frustration at the lack of opportunity. Whereas the un-Christian owner would claim everything for himself, the un-Christian worker would set forth the "equally false moral principle," cited by Pius XI: "that all products and profits, excepting those required to repair and replace invested capital, belong by every right to the workingman." Actually, there is no difference in the *spirit* of either man; both are un-Christian, differing only by the fact that one is the owner and the other a worker. This spirit will help no one.

This is no small task that lies before the Christian workers of the world. They must strive to make their fellow-workers see that their labor is not a necessary evil, but a part of God's divine plan. The hardships they endure can become a means of sanctifying themselves, of sanctifying the world. There is, after all, very little difference between the work of Christ in His carpenter shop, and that of a modern worker in his. And there should be no difference in the spirit in which they work, although there often is. It is the spirit of Christ that makes the difference. This Christian ideal of equality, of unity in Christ, forms the best foundation for a harmonious society. "Then only will it be possible to unite all in harmonious striving for the common good," warns Pius XI, "when all sections of society have the intimate conviction that they are members of a single family and children of the same Heavenly Father; and further, that they are 'one body in Christ and everyone members one of another.' Workingmen, too, will lay aside all feelings of hatred or envy, which the instigators of social strife arouse so skillfully. Not only will they cease to feel weary of the position assigned them by Divine Providence in human society; they will become *proud* of it, well aware that every man by doing his duty is working *usefully and honorably for the common good,* and is following in the footsteps of Him, Who, being in the form of God, chose to become a Carpenter among men, and to be known as the Son of a Carpenter."

The individual Christian must, naturally, let the love of Christ show forth in his daily life. For all practical purposes, that worker *is* Christ for the mass of nonbelievers at his side. He must show by his word and his example just what it means to be a Christian, by his concern for the trials of his fellow workers, by his interest in their lives, and by his zeal in procuring their good, he must be another Christ. This will call for self-sacrifice; it calls for *personal dedication,* even to the point of forgetting self. Christ, indeed, has given us an example not only of toil but of self-immolation; His members cannot give less than He, by His example, has asked. "Undoubtedly the first and immediate apostles of the workingmen must themselves be workingmen, while the apostles of the industrial and commercial world should themselves be employers and merchants." These words of Pius XI touch the very heart of this modern apostolate. If the workers fail to make Christ live in themselves and in those about them, they will be failing in their mission as members of Christ's Body.

On the other hand, those who would stop the worker at this individual apostolate fail to grasp the whole problem. The worker is not merely an individual; he is part of a world, and to transform the spirit of that world, he must join forces with others. There is no other way. A worker may complain about the hideous atmosphere in which he is forced to work: the conversation treats of nothing but sex; foul language and filthy jokes are the order of the day; and indecent pictures cover the walls. His life lacks security, his wages are not in just proportion to the profit, his safety is not considered. He finds himself, in short, in that strangely perverted system described by Pius XI where "dead matter leaves the factory ennobled and transformed, but where men are corrupted and degraded." Some Christians might advise him to "bear patiently" these wrongs. One man answered, for example, by way of a little story. "Last year," he said, "I happened to be traveling in a very ugly section of our country. The homes were broken down, dirt covered everything. And off to one side, there was a large coalyard, scattering its black dust far and wide. But off in one little corner, I saw a lonely little daffodil. Its pale yellow color seemed like a ray of hope in all that sordid blackness, and I thought how true it is that no matter how bad things are, we may still find a touch of beauty in it all. Try and look upon your life like that. It can be a thing of beauty, despite what you see on all sides of you."

As a temporary measure, this is good advice. In the long run, however, we must soon realize that we will have to stop trying to be a yellow daffodil in a coalyard if we are to be true Christians. Our faith must be an apostolate, a community-minded apostolate. "Isolated, the Christian is an island in an ocean of indifference," writes Cardinal Suhard. "Even if he himself remains faithful, society does not get the full benefit of his services." The eminent Cardinal termed this tendency the "temptation of Thabor." When Christ was transfigured on this mountain before Peter, James, and John, Peter cried out: "Master, it is good for us to be here." But we cannot stay there. The Christian community must not become a closed group, forgetful of the mission entrusted to it of transforming the world. The worker must not be satisfied with being a good worker himself; he must exercise his influence upon the entire field to which he belongs, and as he cannot do that alone, he must unite with others.

Experience has taught men one thing: this is not a task for the individual alone. Modern life is socialized; it is organized. The forces of antichrist have banded together to win the workers of the world, and to promote unrest in their ranks. The members of Christ must meet them on the same level. Some men fail to see this; they cannot understand the justice of a labor union; they cannot understand the reason why a pope should write a labor encyclical.

To such men, these measures seem to indicate an obvious interference of religion in the affairs of life, and we can only answer that that is exactly what it is. Religion was *meant* to interfere in the whole of life, except that "interfere" is not the right word. One can interfere only in a place where he has no right to be. Christ *intends* to influence everything in life, and He has *every right* to do so; His religion must do the same. The enemies of religion would like to confine the Church to the sacristy; it would leave the field free for the planting of their own religion of unbelief. This is especially true in the field of labor. The Catholic must not stand by idly, watching the Communist-inspired worker take over the labor union. As another Christ, he cannot allow men of godless ideals to surpass him in expressing his concern and his sympathy for the needs of the worker. There is a world of difference between the Christian and the Communist ideal. The Communist would use the labor union to destroy the capitalist. He would use it, as he uses every possible means, to bring about a "classless" society. He foments unrest among the worker in order to bring about this clash, this conflict which must precede the forming of a Communistic society. In what appears to be a defense of the workers' rights, he will turn to all forms of injustice; in his efforts to destroy the owner, he will revert to gangster tactics. Christ would not approve of such a movement by any means. He would be concerned for the safety of the worker and the preservation of his rights. He knows that the worker must feel that he is important for society; he must retain his sense of personal dignity. But Christ would also realize that the Communist would do just the opposite. He would destroy not only capital but labor as well, erasing every individual life by identifying men with "The State."

Because of this, the members of Christ's Mystical Body must take an interest in the problems of labor. They cannot retire to the sacristy, and leave the labor unions to the leftist agitators and Communist cells. They have a real obligation to play an active roll in the program of labor movements. The apathy of some Christian workers in this regard is alarming. The true Christian simply cannot stand by and watch a group of unscrupulous labor leaders destroy the investment of a man, totally against the principles of justice. He cannot ignore the unsound labor tactics which would destroy the business of the investor and owner, and the jobs of the workers eventually. Yet such are the tactics of the Communistic idealist who would hope only to destroy both capital and labor and then permit "The State" to take over for both. He cannot stand quiet and refuse to show others that they are not helping the interest of the worker in the long run, but only harming him. "It is impossible to reduce human society to a level," wrote Leo XIII. "The Socialists may do their utmost, but all striving against nature is vain. . . . Those who hold out to a hard-pressed people freedom from pain and trouble, undisturbed repose, and constant enjoyment, cheat the people, and impose upon them; their lying promises will only make the evil worse than before." The members of Christ's Mystical Body must see that Christ's spirit is present even within labor unions: His spirit of justice, of honor. They must see that the promises held out are not vain promises; they must see that their fellow workers are not *deluded* into promoting a final goal they do not want because of "short-time" promises of what they do want. Here especially would Christ the Worker speak out today. His members have possibly been too silent already. They have permitted the Communist to show more love and concern than they. If they continue, their silence will serve only to promote the cause of evil.

The members of Christ in the field of labor have a tremendous task laid before them. It involves influencing men's minds and their hearts and bringing about a change in the conditions in which they live. In this way only will our modern industrial world feel the presence of Christ; only then will our factories and offices become places where Christ may labor without embarrassment; only then will the rights of capital be defended by the justice of Christ. Only in the way of Christ will the worker regain his rightful place in society without destroying, as would the Communist, the nature of society itself and the dignity of the individual.

Christ the Worker must live on in the world. He must live in the foundry worker, the man on the assembly line, the construction crew, the telegraph operator, the bus driver, the grocery clerk. From a thousand desks in a thousand offices, the prayer of Christ must ascend, day by day, to the accompaniment of a thousand typewriters and the click of a thousand pencils. Throughout all these fields, Christ must live. His spirit of dedication, His spirit of love, His spirit of social union, of justice and equality, must reign. A Christian who works is not simply a man who happens to have a job; nor is he a revolutionary seeking to reduce society to a common level. He is *Christ,* working hour after hour, sending up to the eternal throne the pledge of His labor; He is Christ, joining all mankind under His headship, and promoting the reign of God and His justice upon earth; Christ reciting in every man that constant prayer of the Christian heart: *Thy kingdom come.*

CHAPTER XIV

THE FARMER

*Behold, the sower went
out to sow. . . .*

THERE is one sphere of human life about which Christ spoke very frequently, although He Himself had never engaged in that work. It is the work of the farmer. Time after time, Christ turned to rural life for examples with which to clothe His message. The people of the Holy Land were well acquainted with these various scenes of the countryside, so that the parables of Christ were most timely. But more than that, Christ realized that certain closeness to God which marks the life of the farmer; it was this that made these parables so fitting. It is not difficult to pass from the tender regard of the shepherd for his flock to the enduring love of God for men. When we see how much the farmer's work depends upon the gifts of God, we can more easily understand how much our souls depend upon His grace as well. And when we see the branch wither away as soon as it falls from the vine, we can see how quickly we ourselves will perish apart from Christ.

There is, perhaps, no work on earth more admirably suited to keep a man in the presence of God — no work so close to the power of God as that of a farmer. It would seem that Christ would find it very easy to live on in His members who do this work; the interest of Christ in things rustic should continue for all time because there would be other Christs devoting their life to that vocation. Yet, what do we find? The sacredness of rural life has been too largely forgotten. Thousands, all over the world, have left the farm, and turned to the city. Those who have remained behind have done so, only too frequently, because they feel they were trapped; they spend their days trying to be as "citylike" as they can. The modern tendency to look down upon manual labor has affected not only our attitudes toward the factory worker and the artisan; it has struck at the dignity of farm labor as well, so much so that a man might almost feel that he ought to apologize for being a farmer. It is an amazing reversal of fact! It is our cities that have contributed most to the lowering of man's dignity; it is in their factories especially that "bodily labor," which was decreed by Providence for the good of man's body and soul even after original sin, has everywhere been changed into an instrument of strange perversion: where "dead matter," as Pius XI remarked, "leaves the factory ennobled and transformed, where men are corrupted and degraded." Rather than sharing this spirit of the city, it is the special mission of those members of Christ who live on the land to lead their fellow men out of this confusion; they especially have an opportunity to restore to manual labor the dignity that belongs to it.

The farmer still has many of the things that the city laborer needs to regain his dignity in work. If only he will realize it! He possesses a reasonable freedom and security; most often he either owns or is gradually acquiring ownership of his own property; he knows what personal responsibility is, and how necessary it is to preserve human personality in work; he has an opportunity for good spiritual and physically healthful conditions for his family. He has an opportunity to partake in a fairly permanent village social life, and a chance to live a full spiritual life on the social level — on the liturgical level. His very life can lead him to be increasingly aware of his dependence upon God; the traditional neighborliness of rural life is a continued reminder of the dependence of men upon one another. These are benefits for which he may thank God daily. They place him in a position where he can demonstrate to the entire world what a true Christian life should be. By making Christ live in his particular segment of society, he can hope that his "city cousins" will pattern their life on his, rather than the reverse.

There is no question, of course, of everyone walking out of the cities and taking to the farms. The city is here to stay. Most city men, moreover, would only starve more quickly on the farm than they might, at present, in the city. It is partially, however, a question of stopping the mass exodus from the country into the city. There is a need for more people on our farms, and there is opportunity for them there. Those men and women who are able to do so, should turn to that way of life. If rural life is ever to become the great Christian example in our day, there must first of all be larger numbers of people who turn to that life willingly, freely, joyfully. There must be men and women who will not feel that they are simply "stuck" down on the farm, and who try to make the best of the situation; there must be men and women who will be *proud* of their vocation as farmers, and who will realize the opportunity which is theirs of helping to bring Christ back into human life.

The life of a man in the city cannot hope to copy the rural life in every detail; there must be adaptation at all times. With an example set before him, however, of what life *could* be, he will more easily give up the false ideals of an industrial age; he will more quickly set about making that adaptation, interpreting what he has seen in terms of his own life and circumstances. Our cities are far from God, but they can be brought back. The streetcars and the skyscrapers, the boulevards and the apartment houses, the noisy streets and the factories can all be made to contribute to the image of Christ living among men. But the farm, though far away, is closer to God; it cannot shut out nature. Its journey, then, is shorter; it can find God again more quickly. The essence of a Christian is to be a witness; he leads not so much by his words as by his life. If the cities have been blamed for leading men away from God, it may be that by seeing Christ living fully in our rural areas, they will find Him again.

The farmer builds his Christian life upon the same foundations that any man must use. There is first and foremost an utter dependence upon God. The farmer can see this more easily because the wind and the rain and the sun are constant reminders of God, of our dependence upon His gifts. The birds of the air and the flowers in the field speak to him of God; the wheat ruffled by the breeze whispers of a Power that is beyond the power of man. In the city, the God of nature is more easily hidden. The air is filled with factory smoke, and buildings, one upon another, blot out the sun; the trees and the flowers give way to concrete walks, and the song of the bird is drowned out by the noise of automobile horns. Yet the man of the city must find God where he is; he must see God in the city: the majesty of God in the hugeness of buildings, the power of God in the sound of the factory, the presence of God in the hustling crowd.

Next to this, there comes the dignity of man. The city laborer is striving to regain that dignity: the right to be treated as a human being and not as a machine. The farmer, however, can again lead the way because his life can possess that personal responsibility so important for retaining human dignity. He does not simply bolt on a left fender as an assembly line of somebody else's cars passes by; he is harvesting *his* grain, tending *his* cattle. Even if he is only working for another, the farmer has a sense of personal accomplishment. He has watched the field grow under his hand; there is more in his view of life than a left fender.

Cities have been charged with being breeders of vice and disease — a charge that cannot be entirely written off as prejudice. The crowded conditions of our large cities, the tenements, the poverty have contributed to the decline of health. In this, the farmer stands at a definite advantage, as a rule. Spiritually, freedom from observation and general indifference toward others have helped men to indulge in a lower moral standard in city life. Men feel that they can "get away" with more in such a situation. Naturally, the moral standards of large numbers of people are the same, whether in the city or the country; there are saints and sinners in both areas. The small community of the rural area, however, does serve as a deterrent, and this can be of no little help in fashioning a Christian community. In the life of the city, this concern for the common good and the resultant concern for the general moral standard must be created; the spirit of individualism is a hindrance in this regard.

The social spirit also shows itself in rural life in the general attitude of neighborliness; it is a good steppingstone to a spirit of oneness in Christ. We often hear others remark on how "cold" and "unfriendly" people are in the city, and how much different they find those in the country. The man who lives in the city must become somewhat indifferent toward others as a defense; he is pressed in by humanity on all sides. He, then, will perhaps have a more difficult time forming an ideal of our social union in Christ; but once again, he can learn from his friends in the country. There is a reason why men tend to be more indifferent in a city, but there is no reason why city life *must* follow that pattern. If that were true, Christianity could never be the social bond in cities that it must be. But farmers are accustomed to helping their neighbor; harvesttime will find many of them passing from farm to farm, aiding one another. This spirit has great meaning in developing a Christian community as well.

Even the very social life of the country has its advantages in this regard. The community is fairly stable, whereas in the city there is often an endless series of neighbors moving in and out. People live for years in the same block without ever knowing even the names of most of their neighbors; many even live in the same building without knowing one another. Social life in the city has a more difficult time taking root, but again, it is something that is needed to refashion society.

Above all, of course, the renewal of society must begin in the parish; the men and women who form the parish must become conscious of their own oneness in Christ before they can go out to transform the world about them. And here also, we see that the country areas have a remarkable advantage. Parish life there, like social life, is fairly stable. People can know one another; they can learn to work with one another. Especially, however, can they learn to pray together with an ease that is not often experienced in city parishes. The liturgical life can expand in a country parish far more easily because of that. The same people will meet in the same church each week at the same hour; what an opportunity that is for the introduction of the dialogue Mass and congregational singing. A city parish often labors under the handicap of a constantly changing membership. Different people turn up at different hours each week, even in different churches. It adds to the difficulty of liturgical participation. Not that it makes it impossible; by no means. But for leadership and example, the members of the Church may justly look to the rural areas where there are fewer obstacles and so much to promote the liturgical life.

Every Christian must take his role in the task of Christianizing the world. We must all do whatever we can to make Christ live in our own little part of the world. Christ must live in us as individuals. He must live in our homes, but also in our communities. Christ must, through His members, live in our cities; He must live in the rural areas no less. Those men and women who are farmers will naturally be the apostles in that field. They will, as a matter of course, turn their energies toward bringing the principles of Christ into their "world." His honesty, His integrity, His spirit of social justice must reign in the country as well as the city. Social legislation and economic progress will naturally form a part of their concern; the advances and the methods of modern science will also help lighten their burden.

The farmer, however, is in a position to do something that others cannot so easily accomplish toward Christianizing the entire world. He can help all men to regain the notion of the sanctity of labor; he can help them realize that no one works "for himself." The farmer living in the most isolated corner of our country is not working only for his own good, but for the good of society. He grows food for the world. He must know that, and help spread that social consciousness.

Above all, these Catholics in rural areas must live their faith vitally, firmly, intelligently; they must be a pattern of the social worship of the Church, and an example in social living. Christ once made frequent use of the countryside to bring home to His hearers the full import of Christian truth. Today, He would ask these members to be *living parables*. He would ask them to go forth and sow the seed of Christian life in their own communities, and in this way reap a harvest throughout the world.

CHAPTER XV

THE CHRISTIAN IN WAR

But when you hear of wars and rumors of wars,
do not be alarmed;
for they must come to pass,
but the end is not yet. . . .

IN THESE days of social unrest, the Christian is faced with confusing situations. Not the least of them is war. Our times have been times of warfare; whole generations have been born into the world during the course of one war, only to die on the battlefield of the next. How utterly un-Christian it seems. When we talk about every member of Christ's Mystical Body being another Christ, we might have difficulty understanding how this could be true when a man goes to war. What could Christ, "meek and humble of heart," possibly have to do with warfare? Should we not say that when a man enters into military service, he ceases, temporarily, to mirror Christ in what he does?

The attitude of the Christian, however, will ultimately be that of Christ. He is against war, for Christ came as the Prince of Peace; and yet he knows that not all men will freely submit to the love of our Lord. The following of Christ is a completely free act; not even God Himself will force the human will. It is the perversity of human nature that causes wars; they arise in direct proportion to man's rejection of God. Thus, even though it is something completely against his way of life, the Christian will occasionally find that war is a situation with which he is faced. It is something thrust upon him by a particular set of circumstances, and he then finds it necessary to continue to act in a Christian way. Where normally the followers of Christ would mirror His mildness and His patience, they must now show forth His righteous indignation and His defense of justice.

A Christian does not seek war, but when he is faced with it, he accepts it as something that is "there." When all his other efforts fail, and he has no choice left, he approaches the battlefield to defend his rights. The justification of war comes from the same principles of justice that permit an individual to defend his own life, his own family, his own possessions. A country has those same rights; it may defend those rights, and even prepare beforehand for any possible attack upon them.

When Christ foretold that "nation will rise against nation, and kingdom against kingdom," He was not causing those wars; He was merely facing a situation as it would be. War, like crime, remains a witness to at least the partial failure of Christianity — the failure of Christians to introduce the fullness of their way of life into the lives of men in general. But that means, more concretely, the failure of some individual men to preach Christ and the refusal of others to accept Him. "The peace of Christ in the reign of Christ" implies that peace flows from the acceptance of our Lord; Christ must first reign. The very best way to prevent warfare is to spread the truth of Christ far and wide, and to increase His reign among men. All efforts for peace that leave Christ and religion out of the picture are doomed to failure. Men, both as individuals and as societies, are wounded and sick; Christ is the *only* cure.

The pacifist would reverse the solution; he envisions the peace of Christ even among those who have rejected the reign of Christ. For that reason, his is an unreal solution; it fails to meet the situation as it really is. It is an idealistic outlook, but unreal. Christ did ask His followers to suffer patiently the evils that should befall them; and He said: "Love your enemies, do good to those who hate you, and pray for those who persecute and calumniate you." But He would not have them give up their sense of right judgment. It is one thing to accept grievances patiently and quite another thing to be walked over. Pacifism is a doctrine of the heart, of the emotions, because it tends to turn its back on the realities of life. Wars have been fought for centuries; the battles of 1918 were fought "to end all wars." None but the most sanguine can hope, as they view that failure, that our present conflicts will bring such perfect deliverance. To be sure, there *is* this peace which will last: the peace of Christ in the reign of Christ. But we must first set up the reign of Christ in the hearts of men. To cast away all manner of defense while endeavoring to refashion the hearts of men, would be to give way to emotion. By confusing our early attempts with the achievement of our goal, we would be closing our eyes to reality. We would do no more than leave open the road to conquest for those who still know no other God than the "god of might," who makes his own right. The simple fact remains that there are such men in the world. When we see our homes, our faith, our way of life endangered by their onslaughts, we have a duty to defend what is ours. When we see that they would overtake us by force, and thrust their godless views upon us by unscrupulous indoctrination of ourselves and our children, we certainly are not well advised to cast down our weapons, and let those ruinous evils come upon us.

All of this means that wars may be, and sometimes are, fought not only for political or economic reasons, but as a defense of the Christian way of life. Perhaps at no time in the New Testament era has this been more obvious than in our own days. Interwoven with all the mixed reasons for war in the past, both good and bad, there was frequently the desire to preserve the Christian culture from the attacks of pagan or Moslem forces. The ideologies that have fashioned our modern dictatorships, however, have stressed from the outset the need of crushing all religion. We realize today the sad truth of what Pius XI proclaimed in 1937: "Communism is intrinsically wrong, and no one who would save Christian civilization may collaborate with it in any undertaking whatsoever." And at that time, he was simply repeating the declaration of his predecessor, Pius IX, issued as early as 1846, in which he condemned "that infamous doctrine of so-called

Communism which is absolutely contrary to the natural law itself, and if once adopted would utterly destroy the rights, property and possessions of all men, and even society itself."

Each war presents its own individual moral problem, and there certainly have been unjust wars. The lax Christian, despite his faith, has fought freely and willingly. Many other Christians have been forced against their wills, to engage in battle. They are victims of power politics, and perhaps more than anything else, they reflect the suffering and resignation of Christ in what they do. There have been many members of Christ's Mystical Body who have been forced to fight on the side of a government whose ideology they did not accept; others fought with less inner conflict because they had been deceived about the true nature of those political beliefs. But there are now, and have been in the past, those who have fought to defend the rights of men and God: defenders of Christianity and the Christian way of life. While we cannot say that every war is justified, we would do wrong to pass to the opposite extreme, and say that no war is ever just. We might only wonder what turn our civilization might have taken had German Nazism carried the day. Seeing what is happening now in those places where Communists have gained control, we can only shudder at the thought of what the final outcome might be, should their victory be complete. Far more than military victory is at stake.

The Christian soldier, then, can take up the cause of Christ. If he gains an insight into the real and ultimate issues for which he fights, he will know that he is fighting for principle. The right of war stems from man's natural right to defend his life, his possessions, his homeland against unjust aggression. Christianity would seek to refashion the hearts of all men so that they might live in peace; surely if all men were filled with the spirit of Christ, there would be no unjust aggressors. But Christianity would not deprive men of their natural right to defend what is theirs, even if the roots of Christian civilization itself are not involved in the conflict. When Christianity itself is actually involved, the right is all the more obvious. If Christian truth be taken away, and godless hate implanted in its stead, life itself will lose its meaning.

The militarist is certainly not a man with the mind of Christ. Far more accurately, it is the rejection of God that is the ultimate cause of such a mentality. Not all men have accepted the rule of Christ as yet, nor, we may suppose, will they in the future. And it is the man who trusts in himself rather than God who will seek military might; it is he who will remain a constant threat to civilization. It was because of this that Pius XII said in 1951: "All, taught by bitter experience, unfortunately know that, in the hard reality of the present hour, even the most sincere love of peace cannot overlook alert vigilance against the danger of unjust aggression." The sad but realistic conclusion that the world today has reached is that indulgence, timidity, and meekness encourage the aggressor and increase the threat of war; that we can deal with dictators only through strength, if we wish to dispose of conflicts peacefully.

In this light, we can see the mind of Christ even in those whose work must be the bloody business of war. A standing army, like a police force, will remain a part of human life because of those who refuse Christ. Members of Christ's Mystical Body must, however, assume the role of Christ even in their military life. They must be the men who will keep alive those Christian ideals for which our forces would fight. Should our armies lose sight of these, we would pass quickly down the road of militarism; we would be tempted to look upon our military power as an end in itself rather than a means to achieve the lasting goal of peace.

Besides bringing into military circles the ideals of Christ, the followers of our Lord must also bring His virtues. It will do little good to send armies to fight in defense of our Christian way of life, if military life itself is bent on destroying Christian virtue. If the members of Christ's Mystical Body must do what they can to Christianize the lives of their fellow men in factories and offices and schools, there is no reason to deny that obligation in the case of a military man. Only too many young men and women look upon entrance into the army or navy as an excuse for abandoning their Christian ideals and embarking upon an extended fling of immorality. Overcoming this is certainly not a task for the army alone. The men who come to the service carry with them the views of their civilian life. A society that boasts of its low moral tone and broken families can hardly present the armed forces with well-trained recruits. But those men in the military life, who are members of Christ's Mystical Body, must do what they can to see that army life does not fall lower at least than the level of civilian life. There is that danger. Freed of the restraints of family and public opinion, the young serviceman might come to think of his life in the service as a time of "manly" debauchery. The conversation, the spirit of the barracks might do little, unfortunately, to disabuse him of that notion.

On the other hand, the army man can do much to elevate the moral level of his associates, if only he will. There is a real Christian vocation resting upon those who undertake military life. The purpose of the Church is to make Christ's presence felt in those places where it is needed. The army or navy is certainly no exception. Even more, military life offers an unusual opportunity for exercising a Christian influence upon others, for the followers of Christ bring with them much that is needed in the difficulties of such a life — much that others do not have. They bring with them Christian idealism first of all; they bring the means of living up to those ideals: the Sacraments, the Mass. In the intimate circles of military life, men have a tremendous opportunity to influence the lives of their associates, provided they seize the opportunity. While it is true that many men have come out of the service less fit morally than when they entered, there are thousands who have *gained* from their experience. The difference lies in those disciples of Christ who either live up to their vocation as "other Christs," or abandon it. No less than the priest in civilian life, the chaplain alone cannot Christianize military life. The obligation of spreading the influence of Christ rests upon the members of the laity as well.

The Christian soldier also has an opportunity to mirror the virtues of Christ in what he does. His is the bravery of Christ, the courageous heart of Christ. In union with our suffering Lord, He can show those about him the Christian way of enduring hardship, the cheerful acceptance of suffering and death. As he mounts a barren hilltop, he does not walk alone; Christ is with him, Christ is in him. Christ the lone, the weary; Christ suffering and afraid; Christ the Strength of the helpless and the Defender of the weak. Christ must ride the seas in the defense of justice. He must take to the air in those who are His members, to protect the poor and the oppressed. The justice of Christ, the love, the patience, the heroism of Christ must live in His members in the armies of the world. The goal is not military victory alone, but peace. But there is only one peace that will endure: the peace of Christ in the reign of Christ; and even in this sad and bloody means of achieving peace, Christ must be ever present, lest any of us should lose sight of that final goal; lest, for even a moment, we should lose sight of that shining image of Christ ever calling out to mankind: "Peace I leave with you, my peace I give to you."

CHAPTER XVI

THE CHRISTIAN EXECUTIVE

You know that those who are regarded
as rulers among the Gentiles
lord it over them, and their great
men exercise authority over them.
But it is not so among you. . . .

IN THESE days of democracy, the rulers of the world have assumed a more benign attitude, for their power depends upon the vote of the people. But the desire to rule remains strong among the kings of the economic field, and it is at that point that Christianity meets one of its greatest problems. The tendency to "lord it over them," is a tendency common to all of mankind. Any smallest bit of power or authority is liable to produce a fresh outpouring of such pride. Even the youngster who is appointed a school prefect will tend to use his newly gained power for his own glory rather than the promotion of the common good. This is all the more true when vast "kingdoms" of commercial or industrial wealth are concerned. And yet no problems of labor can be solved without considering the interests and the rights of those who are on the side of capital.

Once again, Christ must live in those of His members who are engaged in the work of business. He does this with full right. Indeed, during His life upon earth, He freely chose to be among the poor: "The Son of Man has nowhere to lay his head." At the same time,

He was the Ruler of the Universe; He possessed everything although He had nothing. He may speak, then, both by word and example of how the man having great possessions should act.

Christ spoke very frequently of the "poor in spirit." It should be noted, however, that, in doing so, He was not condemning wealth and possessions as such. A millionaire can be very poor in spirit; a penniless tramp can be just the opposite: he can be very attached to things of the world. Perhaps St. Paul expressed the mind of Christ better than anyone else when he spoke of those "who buy, as though not possessing; and those who use this world, as though not using it, for this world as we see it is passing away."

There is even a difference, too, between the man with great possessions and the man who runs his own, but rather small business. A man who owns his own grocery store is a businessman, but very often he has as much to fear from "big business" as the ordinary laboring man. The details of his problems, however, differ from those of the worker and the great capitalist, and it is for this reason that we find no easy solution to our economic problems. Communism attempts to solve all problems by eliminating them; in place of the worker, the businessman, or the capitalist, Communism would insert "The State" in each case. Men then lose all rights as individuals, and one problem is solved only by the creation of another, far greater problem.

There are certain fundamental principles that Christianity would never deny. Foremost among these is the right of ownership on the part of the individual. Whether a man owns a house or a plot of land, an automobile or a television set, he has a right to call it *his own;* if life has brought him a great accumulation of wealth, he has a right to that no less. "Thus it is clear," wrote Leo XIII, "that the main tenet of Socialism, the community of goods, must be utterly rejected. . . . Our first and most fundamental principle, therefore, when we undertake to alleviate the condition of the masses, must be the *inviolability of private property.*" He warns further that "it is impossible to reduce human society to a level. The Socialists may do their utmost, but all striving against nature is vain. There naturally exists among mankind innumerable differences of the most important kind; people differ in capability, in diligence, in health, and in strength; and unequal fortune is a necessary result of inequality in condition."

On the other hand, ownership carries with it not only certain rights, but also certain obligations. In the use of his possessions, man does not have unlimited freedom; he must often stop to consider the rights of others, as well as the demands of the common good. This is the ultimate justification of taxation. There is a twofold character to ownership: an individual and a social element. It is in the balancing of these two elements that endless difficulties will arise.

The most basic principle in all such discussions, however, is that stated so clearly by Leo XIII when he wrote: "Capital cannot do without labor, nor labor without capital." To understand this properly, we need to develop a very definite appreciation of the social side of human life. We are all dependent upon one another, and therefore we cannot ignore the claims of any one party when distributing our wealth. In cases where, as today, many men are not applying their labor to their own property, "an alliance must be formed between his toil and his neighbor's property," as Pius XI remarks, "for each is helpless without the other. . . . It is entirely false to ascribe the results of their combined efforts to either party alone; and it is flagrantly unjust that either should deny the efficacy of the other and seize all the profits."

History does not, unfortunately, hold too favorable a record of the economic practices of those who possessed great wealth. Even within Catholic circles, certain employers and industrialists failed openly. "They refused," as Pius XI lamented, "to understand that Christian charity demands the recognition of certain rights due to the workingman, which the Church has explicitly acknowledged." Their opposition to these principles was so obvious that mention of it found a place in a papal encyclical. "What is to be thought of the action of those Catholic employers," asked Pius XI, "who, in one place, succeeded in preventing the reading of Our Encyclical *Quadragesimo Anno* in their local churches? Or those Catholic industrialists who even to this day have shown themselves hostile to a labor movement that We Ourselves recommended? Is it not deplorable that the right of private property defended by the Church should so often have been used as a weapon to defraud the workingman of his just salary and his social rights?"

As Pius XI had already written: "Capital was long able to appropriate to itself excessive advantages; it claimed all the products and profits and left to the laborer the barest minimum necessary to repair his strength and to ensure the continuation of his class. By an inexorable economic law, it was held, all accumulation of riches must fall to the share of the wealthy, while the workingman must remain perpetually in indigence or reduced to the minimum needed for existence."

This is a realistic, if sad, view of things as they were. If it has seemed that those of wealth have been asked to go *more* than halfway in solving our modern problems, it is only because the rich men of an earlier era went far *beyond* that halfway mark in taking to themselves the profits of industry. It is not easy to restore the proper balance. Today's men find themselves burdened with an economic problem not entirely of their own making; it is something that was forged in ages past.

By way of reaction, however, the claims of labor have at times been set forth in "another equally false moral principle," as Pius XI also notes: "that all products and profits, excepting those required to repair and replace invested capital, belong by every right to the workingman." This goes too far. Admittedly, the underprivileged worker has been in greater need of defense in modern times; he lacks the power of wealth to defend himself. But today, with the mighty arm of the labor union at his disposal, a new element is added. The worker's lot is better, but with the increased power of his class, there is also an ever increasing danger of injustice on the side of the worker. He may seek too much; in seeking his own goals, he may violate the principles of justice.

In between these two extremes, we may hope for the proper *balancing* of products and profits, avoiding the evils of both Collectivism and Individualism. It is in the seeking of that balance that the Christian has the most to offer. If he fails to contribute his own Christian insights, he shirks his obligation. As Leo XIII pointed out long ago, "no practical solution of this question will ever be found without the assistance of Religion and the Church." Christianity is not a pious hobby; it is something essential to mankind in its present state. It is not easy for a man of wealth to give up the attitudes current in our modern-day world. He has most probably been reared in an atmosphere of individualism, where he has come to think that he can settle all questions by answering that "What is mine, is mine." We can imagine the amazed reactions of many men when Leo XIII began to speak of these problems in 1891. It was an age when industrial development had reached the stage where the wealth of the world was in the hands of the few, while the many endured a lot little better than slavery. Men of wealth were far more inclined to regard such a situation at that time as something *inevitable*. They looked to charity to relieve the condition of the unfortunate men and women and children who were in need — as if charity could make up for the open violation of justice. Even today, after sixty years of social legislation throughout the world, plus tremendous advances in social thinking, the words of Leo XIII sound like the words of a fanatic to large numbers of men, even Christian men.

Yet, approaching the current situation honestly, the fact still faces us that the world sees a most unjust distribution of wealth, and — in the long run — there is only *one* way of remedying the situation. No matter what techniques be used, the man of wealth will eventually possess less of that wealth than formerly. Whether it be by taxes, social legislation, revolution, or free-willed social justice, it can add up to nothing more. There is no way of solving these problems without asking more of the man of wealth. His vast fortunes, often untouched throughout a lifetime, and unneeded even for the continuance and betterment of his business, cannot be ignored when another man and his family are actually living from day to day, from hand to mouth.

Perhaps that is why, in certain circles, the Church today is often accused of favoring the poor and the worker against the rich — the same Church that is, at other times and places, no less falsely accused of favoring the rich. The Church, however, like Christ, is a Mediator. She is neither the Church of the rich nor the Church of the poor; she is the Church of all. She stands between all men, to reconcile them, and unite them in Christ. The men and women throughout the world who *are* that Church must constantly seek to achieve that goal. They must steadfastly refuse to make their own that great mistake of society pointed out by Leo XIII: "that class is naturally hostile to class; that rich and poor are intended by nature to live at war with one another."

It is a matter of approach, and until labor and capital join hands for their common good, in a spirit of true and heartfelt brotherhood, the ideal will not be attained. Social legislation that is brought about by struggle and power politics will never solve the evils permanently. Social legislation alone will still leave the *inner spirit* of men untouched. It may represent nothing more than a symbol of simultaneous victory and defeat, with the defeated party simply biding his time until he can reverse the solution to his own advantage. Any true reform in this regard must begin from *within*. It must spring from harmonized co-operation rather than continuous struggle. Without this inner renewal, even the efforts of Christians will appear to be nothing more than pressure politics.

The man of wealth must look further to find his compensations; he must look to his social conscience. It is not an easy task, and if ever the dire need of Christian ideals is seen, it is in this. For him, business must be, as Pius XII points out, "more than a mere means of earning a livelihood." It is more, even, than "technical and practical collaboration of ideas, capital and many types of labor; more than a simple — and very praiseworthy — contribution to the carrying out of social justice." For the Christian, "the great misery of the social order is that it is not deeply *Christian* nor really *human,* but only technical and economic. It is not built on what *should be* its basis and the solid foundation of its unity — the common character of men by their nature and through grace." In his efforts, then, to introduce this Christian and human element into all the levels of business, he is endeavoring to transform mankind "into a society whose members, while differing from one another, constitute, each according to his function, *one united body.*"

There is an apostolate waiting in this field, waiting for the members of Christ who live daily in the realms of business. They alone can solve this problem, because they alone have the means of calming these fears and of giving men the courage to do what is right. Christianity can help the world cast off the shackles of unbridled individualism without falling, at the same time, into the opposite extreme of Communism. There is no social doctrine among men that can even approach the social bonds of the Church of Christ, uniting all mankind in one Mystical Body under the headship of the divine Redeemer.

It is not enough for the Christian to say that he is "against" Communism and false Socialism. He must come forth with his own solution. If he does not, if he retires into a corner to keep his silence, he will be aiding the eventual victory of these false doctrines as truly as if he were preaching them in public. Those men who propose these doctrines know that; that is why they try to silence the members of Christ's Church; that is why they continually try to push them into a corner, telling them "to keep religion out of these affairs."

Christ must live in the plush offices of the busy executive, in the banks and in the stock exchange. His honesty and integrity, His love for His fellow men and His concern for their welfare must be reflected in the daily activities of those engaged in such vocations. They too must "have that mind which was also in Christ Jesus." They must "put on Christ," not only for Sunday, but for every day of the week. They must *be* Christ in what they do.

This is a long way from the limited field that some men would ascribe to religion in life. "To convert the world, however, it is not enough to be saints, and preach the Gospel," in the words of Cardinal Suhard. "Rather one cannot be a saint and live the Gospel we preach without spending himself to provide everyone with the housing, employment, food, leisure, education, etc. — without which life is no longer human." Christianity cannot prosper in a world where so many men are forced to concentrate all their energies on one, sole concern: how to obtain their daily bread in any way they can. Nor can the members of Christ's Mystical Body rest easily as long as these problems continue. They must strive primarily to join all men in the oneness of Christ's Body. Then only will they be able to work out their differences in peace, tempering justice with charity. It is this brotherhood in Christ that offers to the world the one sure means of solving the difficulties of men on all levels of life.

CHAPTER XVII

RECREATION AND THE ARTS

Come apart into a desert place
and rest a while. . . .

ONE of the basic needs of our human nature is that of rest and recreation. We seek it in different ways, each according to his own liking. Some will take part in sports, or watch athletic contests; others will turn to the theater, television, radio, movies; others will choose music or art as a means of escaping from the monotony of daily life. In all these activities, however, the Christian remains always what he is — another Christ. He must enter into his recreation in the spirit of Christ. "Recreation," wrote Pius XI, "in its manifold varieties has become a necessity of people who labor under the fatiguing conditions of modern industry. But it must be worthy of the rational nature of man, and therefore must be morally healthy. It must be elevated to the rank of a positive factor for good, and must seek to arouse a noble sentiment. A people who, in time of repose, give themselves to diversions which violate decency, honor, or morality; to recreations which, especially to the young, constitute occasions for sin, are in grave danger of losing their greatest, even their national power."

Christ would by no means oppose recreation, but He would demand that it be something morally good. So much of the world's recreation reflects the spirit of the world. Men who have no God reflect that in their leisure. There are amazingly large numbers of men and women who need to be taught how to relax in a worth-while fashion; people who need to look beyond sex and drink for means of spending their idle hours. That is one reason for the Christian's interest in recreation; it forms a part of the general problem of making *all* of life Christian.

Recreation, however, must be kept within proper bounds. It must be a relief from our regular duties rather than the principal concern of our lives. To make everything revolve around some free-time activity is a sign of immaturity. A man who thinks of nothing but baseball averages or golf scores or musical comedies or operatic librettos is giving them an importance they do not deserve in his life. The professional baseball player or golfer, the musical-comedy star or opera producer must make these things his concern; that is his work, and as a rule, he regards them as just that. But for the other members of Christ it is especially important to avoid this pitfall, because there is so much to be done; a world is waiting for the message of Christ, and it ill behooves any of us to keep it waiting forever while we play Canasta.

Since a great part of our recreation today consists in watching others perform, there has developed a large group of professionals who make such performances their lifework. It isn't exactly recreation for them. For us attendance at a play now and then affords a pleasant break; but the man who must go through that same performance every night of the week and twice on Wednesdays and Saturdays knows that he has a *job*. Even the professional ball player has days when he would just as soon do anything but play ball; and the concert violinist would often prefer not even to show up at the hall. Yet their work goes on, and since it does, Christ would ask them to be apostles in their own field.

The sportsman, for example, has the obligation of bringing honesty and integrity into his field. He has also the obligation of giving an example of a good Christian life. John Jones, who lives on this street or that, can beat his wife, and drink like mad, and run around with somebody else's wife, but comparatively few will know it. The sport star, however, lives in a goldfish bowl. People know all about him, his likes and his dislikes, his family, his religion, his education; if he beats his wife or gets drunk or is seen with someone else's wife, he causes a sensation. A Christian who accepts the limelight must also realize the heavy demands that are laid upon him; he must reflect the image of Christ even more clearly than the unknown men.

The theater, television, movies, radio all hold a tremendous place of importance in our way of life. For that very reason, they need the spirit of Christ. "It is urgently necessary," said Pius XI, "to make provisions that whatever of God's gifts the progress of the age may have added either to human learning or to technical and scientific skill, shall in this field also be ordained to His glory and to the salvation of souls. . . ." Christ would certainly sanction the use of these inventions for promoting the interests of God. Unfortunately, they are not being so used. The thought of Christ on Broadway, living in members, seems almost blasphemous; we have come to associate Broadway and the theater with sophisticated sin. Nevertheless, since anything that is not bad in itself can be brought to the service of Christ, there is no reason why the entertainment world cannot be brought to Him. That is the mission of Christ's members who are part of that world. They must make Christ's presence felt even there.

The theater and the movie and television world are very much like imaginative literature when they present a story of some sort; the writer really becomes a part of each field, and he carries with him the same opportunities and the same obligations. The story gains added power when it comes to life like this, and for that very reason these fields gain an added importance. They speak in vivid pictures, which the mind absorbs with enjoyment and without fatigue. Even the most untrained of minds can grasp the message of the movie; in place of the effort of reading a book, he need do no more than sit and listen and watch, with the background music telling the story almost without the words. Because of this, Pius XI reminds us that these forms of entertainment "not unlike schools of life, have a powerful influence for good or for evil on the majority of men, more effective than abstract reasoning. Hence they must be made to conform to the aims of the Christian conscience, and prevented from producing effects that are depraving and demoralizing. . . . [They] speak not to individuals but to multitudes, and so in circumstances, time, place, and surroundings which are the most apt to arouse unusual enthusiasm for good as well as for bad, and to conduce to that collective exultation which, as experience teaches us, may assume the most morbid form."

There are dangers in such entertainment, and part of the Christian apostolate lies in warding them off. Just as we must see that immoral books do not flood the market, so we must see that the same type of plays do not take over our stages and screens. We say this is a *part* of that apostolate. As in all else, we cannot be satisfied with doing that, and nothing more. The Christian has more to offer in these fields than a blue pencil with which to cross out filthy words and immoral incidents! There is a *positive* aspect to the apostolate in every imaginable field. The Catholic labor leader is not content with rooting out injustices to the worker or the owner; he comes armed with a positive plan for helping the two to work and live together in harmony. The same thing must be true here. Very possibly we Catholics are too easily satisfied with what we call our task; we feel that we have made real progress if we manage to keep out certain obviously evil situations. Actually, we have just begun at that point. The Church is not a pressure group, but we will have a difficult time convincing others of that until we accept our entire apostolate wholeheartedly; until we go out to tell others what they *should* do, and not simply what they ought *not* do. "Why, indeed, should there be a question of merely avoiding evil?" asks Pius XI; "Why should the motion picture [or television or the theater] simply be a means of diversion and light relaxation to occupy an idle hour? With [their] magnificent power, [they] can and must be a light and a positive guide to what is good."

This is a far more engaging task than mere negative censorship, but also a far more difficult one. The members of Christ must create an atmosphere in which such a positive plan could grow, where real wholesome recreation becomes the order of the day, and where Christ may live in His members unashamed. In history, the modern theater has always borne a close connection with the Christian way of life, and many of its greatest works have stemmed from Christian sources.

If such is not the case today, it must be only because the members of Christ have given up that sector to the enemy. But it must not be abandoned. A man need not give up his faith when he turns to the field of entertainment; he needs only to share it with that field.

Music and art also have a special value in life. Like literature and the theater, they offer an interpretation of life; they seek to tell men the meaning of life. Real art is always an interpretation rather than a mere photograph. A symphonic study entitled *The Sea* will never sound exactly like the sea; if it did we might as well have a recording of the sea. It tries to say more. It wants to speak of the majesty of the sea, perhaps, and the littleness of man; or the peace and the calm to be found along its shores. "The essential purpose of art," according to Pius XI, "its *raison d'être,* is to assist in the perfecting of the moral personality, which is man." It aims at helping a man find himself; it raises him up to a new world, as it were, where he may feel the dignity and the destiny that is his.

Because of their lofty nature, music and art were very quickly enrolled in the service of Christianity. The great and lofty themes which Christ came to preach soon found expression in painting and sculpture and musical composition. The events in the life of Christ have been portrayed time and again: the Nativity, the Crucifixion, the Resurrection. What the artist strives to present, however, is not just a photographlike picture of a woman with her infant child. His aim, rather, is to give some feeling of the magnificence and the awe that enwraps that scene; some feeling that this is *God* who lies nestled in her arms; some hint as to the world-shaking event that this apparently ordinary scene really is.

The many masterpieces of music that have gained their inspiration from Christian truth have all had this same goal: to make the hearer feel the import of some certain event, to make him sense its real meaning, and to *draw him* into it, as it were. The cantatas of Bach and his Passions according to St. Matthew and St. John are splendid examples of this blending of music and Scripture. If many people find it hard to appreciate these works today, it is not only because of the difficulty of the music. A world that has lost the meaning of Christianity does not know how to approach a composition that is so wrapped in the Christian spirit. Bach did not simply write a tune and then set religious words to it; his music grew out of the words.

The greatest blending of words and music is to be found in Gregorian chant. This music sprang from the very heart of early Christianity. Its restoration today labors under a twofold burden: it is so different from today's music, and modern man fails, quite often, to grasp all the meaning behind the words. Words, about the time of Mozart, became a rather secondary thing, both in and out of church. Rossini is supposed to have said that if someone would give him a laundry list, he would gladly set it to music. His remark summarizes his own view, as well as that of a good many others. The approach to Gregorian chant, however, is from the other side. The meaning of the words is the primary concern; the music flows from them. Without some notion of the words, the chant becomes almost meaningless. Add to that difficulty a second one just as great, and it is little wonder that Gregorian chant has a hard time becoming popular. Musically, we are used to harmony and regular rhythm; the chant has but one tone, and a rhythm all its own. It strikes our ear rather harshly at first, especially when (as happens frequently enough) we hear it done badly. The chant is in need of musical apostles all its own.

Whatever his field, however, the musician has an opportunity to interpret life for others. Even the popular dance band is expressing emotions of love and joy and sorrow in a rather painted-up fashion. Love in real life may never seem to be the same thing we hear about in the song, but on closer examination there isn't much difference. It does us good to see that. And by the same token, it does us a good deal of harm to hear love sung about as though men and women are nothing but a flock of animals in a perpetual mating season. We cannot help but interpret life whether we sing about it or talk about it or write about it; but whenever we do any of the three, the spirit of Christ should be present to make sure that we do it properly.

The concert artist, the symphony orchestra will try to ennoble the lives of their fellow men by leading them to a world apart, where they can escape for a time and gain a better and clearer insight into

the meaning of life. The artist will try to appeal to the finer instincts of man; he will do a decided favor for the believer if he
presents him with artistic works of religious value; if he can offer
real art to replace the cheap plaster-of-Paris statues which flood the
market at present.

Of them all, however, the church musicians and artists are the
most favored, for they can turn their talent directly to the service
and the worship of God. In the task of fashioning Christ in the
hearts of His members, those who come with art and music in
their hands, come with the most efficient means, this side of grace
and priestly functions. We need works that are truly *artistic,* while
being, at the same time, the outgrowth of a real and lively *faith.*
Christ would make use of them to enter into His flock, to make
them grow in His love. But Christ must first live in those who would
write and perform. His vision, His love, and — as all church musicians
know — His patience are the prerequisites for those who undertake
this life.

CHAPTER XVIII

CHRIST AND POLITICS

---

*Render, therefore, to Caesar
the things that are Caesar's,
and to God the things that are God's. . . .*

CHRIST did not come down upon this earth to establish a worldly kingdom. "My kingdom is not of this world," He answered to Pilate. And yet He was not indifferent to the affairs of State. He urged His followers to respect lawful authority and to live up to their obligations as citizens; He showed this by His example. Christ looked upon the State as an instrument of God's authority, with its own rights and privileges. To "render to Caesar the things that are Caesar's" means just that. Christ did not come to do away with civil governments, nor to take them over; He recognized their lawful position in human life.

Ever since the time of Christ, His Church has had to face the problems raised by the existence of civil authority. Christ indicated a concern for the rights of the State and its obligation toward religion, and so the Church must continue that interest. On the other hand, Christ showed clearly that He did not want to turn the State into a religious body, nor His Church into the State. The things that are God's and the things that are Caesar's must remain separate. And this has raised one of the most difficult problems we know, one that has not been solved perfectly to this day. Even among Catholic theologians there is spirited debate on Church-State relations. But the basic principles are settled beyond dispute. In the first century of the Church, the first Pope repeated the mind of Christ for His followers: "Be subject to every human creature for God's sake, whether to the king as supreme, or to governors as sent through him for vengeance on evildoers and for the praise of the good. . . . Honor all men; love the brotherhood; fear God, honor the king."

State and Church are both supreme in their own order. The State is a perfect society pertaining to the *natural* order; the Church is a perfect society pertaining to the *supernatural* order. They differ according to these orders; they have both come into existence from the hand of God, but they each have a different purpose. Even if Christ had never given a supernatural order to man, nor instituted a Church as a means of sharing in His supernatural gifts, men would have organized themselves politically and formed governments. To do that is natural for man; as a social creature, he simply could not escape such organization. Membership in Christ's Church, however, is not natural to man; that is an honor *superadded* to his human nature. It is a special gift, a supernatural gift; and for that reason the Church is a supernatural organization.

But the Church and State find common ground on one point: they are both made up of *people*. If we said that the Church is above all a group of people, the same is no less true of the State. And it is in the *individual person* that the Church and State will meet. The very same men and women who are members of the Church are also members of the political community. This is, perhaps, the biggest cause of misunderstanding in our present-day disputes. When the newspapers re-echo the charge that the "Pope" wants to move into the White House; or when men claim that "government officials" must either support or repress the Church, there is usually a confusion about the real meaning of both the word "State" and the word "Church."

The Pope is not the Church; nor do the bishops joined with him form the Church. They are a part of the Church — important and essential, but only a part; the Church itself is a group of people, some of whom are rulers and others who are ruled. But together they are the Church. In the same way, a president or a king is not the State; government finds its real meaning in the whole community of men and women who go to make it up. In fact, we should not even talk about the matter until we have a clear idea of what we really mean by the word "State." Since the time of the German philosopher Hegel, there has arisen a rather special notion of the State that is widespread today; it is the notion that the "State" itself is a sort of *superperson.* We might imagine it as a huge monster hovering over a group of men and women. These people form the State, but in so doing, they lose themselves; they exist for the good of "The State" alone. And "The State" speaks through those men who presently possess political power. We have seen such a situation in the reign of Hitler in Germany; we see it today in Communist rule everywhere. It is the deification of the State.

Even Catholics have spoken about the State in a vague fashion in their disputes. They have occasionally said "The State" when they meant "the king" or "the president" or "the senatorial body." As a result, we have been forced to make a number of legal-sounding but highly important distinctions in the words we use, at least when we discuss these problems expressly.

The term *civil society* refers to the sum total of all the different bonds of union between us human beings, uniting us to our fellow men. Some of these do not depend on us at all; they result from the mere fact that we happen to live in a certain region, or speak the same language. On the other hand, we ourselves forge certain *other* bonds; we do so in order to achieve some common purpose. These bonds are then the result of our intellect and free will.

Among the reasons why we freely join ourselves to other men, one of the chief is to promote our common welfare. In this way, we ourselves form the *body politic* or what we call *political society.* "We the people," united in this way, make up that political society; we band together for our common good.

We realize that if our political society is to function correctly, and achieve the purpose we had in mind for it at the start, we must hand over to certain men the power to rule over all of us. A *part* of this political society must specialize in the interests of the whole group;

they must see to it that we accomplish our goal. We call this *the State*. The term refers primarily to something these people *do*. The State is not "somebody." Rather it is an agency made up of experts or specialists in public order and welfare. It is not a man or a body of men; it is a set of institutions combined into a topmost machine by the body politic. It is concerned with maintaining law, promoting the common welfare, and administrating public affairs.

There is, as a result, a relationship between the people and those men to whom they have given such authority; between the rulers and the ruled. When these men put that authority into practice, they set up what we call *government:* a relationship between the two. The people who are ruled by them have, at the same time, given these men that power.

These distinctions might seem rather pedantic, but they are needed. They help us realize why the question is so confusing, and carry a clear warning that we must guard against using carelessly such phrases as "The State is a creature of God" or "The State must worship God." Above all, we must be exact in the meaning of words when we talk about the obligation of the State to support or repress religion and the Church. If we do not, it would be better not to discuss the question, because we are sure to fall into one of two extremes.

We might, first, think that the State is sort of a "superman" to be identified with government officials. We are then faced with two choices: either these men should actively promote the cause of religion, forcing groups of false believers to give up their beliefs; or, we might feel that they should be completely unconcerned about Christ and His religion. Neither solution will really help.

Christ did not intend to make members of His Church through force. His visible representative today, Pius XII, has repeated that fact: "They are most certainly not genuine Christians who against their belief are forced to go into a church, to approach the altar and to receive the Sacraments. . . . Therefore whenever it happens, despite the constant teaching of this Apostolic See, that anyone is compelled to embrace the Catholic faith against his will, Our sense of duty demands that We condemn the act." The Church, as he said at a later date, "does not want to be, and is not, a political power — that is to say, a power which pursues political aims with political means. She is a religious and moral power whose competence reaches as far as the domain of religion and morality — and this domain, in turn, embraces the free, deliberate activity of man, considered either in himself or in society."

The more vaunted opinion today, however, is offered as a solution to these vain fears. Lest the Church control politics, these men contend that the State must be absolutely indifferent to all religion. Their motto is, of course, "Separation of Church and State." What they really mean is "separation of God and society." What they seek is a godless way of life. They complain, therefore, if a public school teacher reads a verse of Scripture at the beginning of her school day. If a Catholic child rides in a school bus, they cry out that this principle of separation has been violated. Logically, we might expect these men to demand that we abolish Thanksgiving Day in America, since it implies giving thanks to God. That is a religious act, and it may embarrass the atheist citizen. And we should, they might say, erase from our coins the very words: "In God we trust." Given time, the proponents of these views will undoubtedly reach such extremes. They have laid special stress upon education, however, because of its importance in forming a national spirit.

Actually, the best path lies between these two extremes. Without confusing the Church and the State, the two must nevertheless work together and help each other. When human beings join together in *civil* society, they cannot forget Christ and Christianity any more than they can ignore Him and His truth in their *private* lives. It is the individual, who is both a citizen of the State and a member of the Church, who draws the two together. In the present state of mankind, no political society can hope to accomplish its task unless the men who constitute it learn to accept the truths of Christianity. Original sin and redeeming grace are facts of history, and if we ignore them, we are really attempting to organize a society of imaginary men. Christ has a role to play on all levels of human society. That is what the popes of all ages have condemned: a civil society that would exclude Christ. Although the State itself belongs to the natural order, it *cannot* go on acting as if there were no supernatural order, no Christ, no Christianity. Christ must live even in the world of politics. Christ must be present there in order to form a *Christian State:* that is, the agency of a political society which collectively acknowledges the rights of Christ; the agency of a group of men and women, politically organized, who accept the rule of Christ, and who endeavor to live according to His precepts in their public and social and political, as well as their personal, lives. In their civil life, these people must accept the Church as something that is "there": as something which God wills to be an essential part of our life in the present order.

The duty of making Christ live in civil society is the special task of the lay members of His Mystical Body. If they show a cold lack of interest in things political, they are going contrary to the example of Christ. He would not have His followers lock themselves up in an ivory tower and let the world fashion its policies without them. *They* have the solution to the problems at hand, and they must exert themselves to apply that solution. The priests and bishops will normally not take an active part in political life; their lives are concerned primarily with spiritual problems and the ruling of this supernatural group, the Church. In rare instances, a member of the clergy may engage actively in political life when no one else is to be found to do so. But if a layman can accomplish the same good, it is his task first of all.

It doesn't take much thought to realize the burden that rests upon those members of Christ's Mystical Body who enter into a life of politics. If they realize that Christ truly lives in them, they will see that they must also make Him live in society. We might even note the obligation resting upon Christians to enter into civil life, when they know that they can accomplish good by so doing. A member of Christ's Mystical Body may be a politician, but he must first and always be a Christian. He can never be just another "politician," in the ugly sense of the word. He must be the man who understands what the supernatural order is. "Separation of Church and State" has a correct meaning, but for the Christian politician, it can never come to mean "separation of the natural and the supernatural order." The supernatural realities (grace, redemption, and the like) envelop the whole natural order; to separate the two would only mean to live as though there were no Christ, no God.

A Catholic who becomes a mayor, an alderman, a senator, or what have you, must know his religion as well as his politics. He has a mission to accomplish in the name of Christ. He must labor for the rights of God and religion in society; and to do that, he must understand his faith. But he must also understand politics. Christ would not have stupid politicians defend His rights, much less dishonest ones. It is here, too, that many of Christ's own members have let Him down. They are the Catholics who have entered into politics and impressed the world only by the extent of their corruption. No follower of Christ can shrug his shoulders and say that, after all, "it's politics." A legislator who seeks his own good or private interests instead of the common good is a poor disciple of Christ. He is not giving "to Caesar the things that are Caesar's"; his is not the mind of Christ. A mayor or a governor who shuts his eye to crime and vice is not "another Christ." Christ does not live in him as He ought. A judge who hands down prejudiced or inaccurate decisions is not helping Christ to live in society; he is not seeking to promote truth and justice after the pattern of Christ. A State Department official or a diplomat who betrays his fellow citizens surely lacks the spirit of Christian loyalty.

We can all try to see Christ in the pope or the priests or in the poor, but to speak of seeing Him in a politician startles us a bit. Yet if there is anything in which Christ professed a concern, His members must mirror that same concern; and political life and justice was a concern of Christ. And if Christ's Church is to accomplish the task laid before it, His members must also help to fashion civil society along Christian lines. The Church seeks to sanctify the individual, and to give to him the mind of Christ. Since that same individual, however, is — at the same time — a member of society, his Christianity must not stop with himself.

"The presence of Christians everywhere is always our clearest command," wrote Cardinal Suhard. The idea of a little group of Christians huddling together to *keep out* the spirit of a pagan world is hardly the ideal of Christ. They must go forth to *put into* the world the spirit of our Lord. "I have come to cast fire upon the earth, and what will I but that it be kindled?" The spirit of Christ was never meant to go no further than the sacristy stove. If the members of Christ should ever shun the world of politics as something "evil," they will be simply limiting the influence of Christ. And because of their neglect, they will share the responsibility for the evils that result, just as truly as though they themselves had introduced them into the world.

CHAPTER XIX

SCIENCE AND RELIGION

When it is evening you say,
  "The weather will be fair, for the
  sky is red.".. .
  . . . You know then how to read the face of the sky,
  but cannot read the signs of the times! . . .

IT HAS often been said by the enemies of religion that the Church is opposed to science and progress. They have carried this opposition so far that they would have a man make a clear-cut choice between the two. "Be a man of faith, or a man of science; but you cannot be both!" It is a puzzling situation. Both theory and practice show that there is no such opposition. There have been thousands of devout Catholics who have been scientists — men like Ampere, Mendel, Marconi, Pasteur. They, like many others, found no real conflict between their faith and their scientific studies; they perceived no insurmountable wall between science and religion. Actually, we ought not expect to find one, because the God of faith is the very same God who created the world which science uncovers. There is no more contradiction between the two than there is contradiction in God Himself. Religion deals with man's relationship to God; it gives an answer to the *why* of life. Science seeks to tell the *how* of life: how the world and men are constituted, how they developed. There is no reason to suppose that the two must clash. Quite the contrary; since they both come forth from God, we should find that they work together in peace and harmony.

As with so many other vocations in modern life, it seems almost shocking to speak of "Christ the Scientist" living in His members. And yet those members of His Church who are scientists are called upon to be other Christs no less than the others; they too must make the presence of Christ felt in the special "world" in which they live. The Christian finds difficulty in accepting the notion that a man of science must hang up his religion with his suit coat as soon as he dons his laboratory smock. Christ would not be unconcerned about the progress of science. Even in His day, He spoke of such little bits of scientific knowledge as the common man possessed. (Such, for example, as the red sky at evening indicating fair weather for the next day.) Even more; when men explain the world in scientific terms today, they are simply telling others what Christ knew from all eternity, "for in Him were created all things in the heavens and on the earth. . . ."

The supposed conflict between science and religion grew up from bad logic rather than from anything else. Scientific knowledge made its greatest advances after the time of the Reformation, and some — very shortsightedly — concluded that it was the Catholic Church which had hindered such advances in the past. In reality, it simply marked the normal growth and development of human knowledge. The advance of science would have gone on even if the Reformation had never been so much as thought of. This type of *post hoc, propter hoc* argument often falls into error. It states that because event number 2 occurred *after* event number 1, it also occurred *because* of event number 1. The Reformation had no more to do with the development of science than, for example, the signing of the Magna Charta had to do with the discovery of America. America was surely discovered after the signing of the Magna Charta, but hardly because of it.

Passing over the large number of Catholics who played an important role in the development of modern science, the enemies of the Church return time and again to the case of Galileo. In point of fact, the treatment of Galileo was merely disciplinary, not doctrinal. Had he confined himself, as he was repeatedly warned, to scientific demonstrations, without meddling with Scripture; and had he proposed his system as probable, rather than as indubitable, he would have excited no opposition. It is rather unfair and even ridiculous to call the Church an enemy of science because she forbids writers to adduce the Scripture in support of their views. A scientist must seek to prove his thesis by scientific methods, and at that time Galileo had not given conclusive proof for what he held. Even some of the greatest scientists of the day, including Francis Bacon, opposed Galileo's views. It can be admitted that the committee of churchmen went too far in condemning Galileo's claims as heretical on the ground that they contradicted Scripture; they were in error. Yet it has been shown too often to bear repetition that their decree was not infallible, nor one by which to determine the official view of the Church toward science.

God has endowed men with intelligence so that they might use it. He would not oppose the proper use of any talent He gave to man. In the ordinary course of events, God would only *expect* that man would turn his attention to the mysteries of the world about him. Why else would He have given man an inquiring mind? And if God Himself would not oppose the advance of human knowledge in scientific matters, much less would His Church upon earth stand in its way. What His Church has opposed, however, is something *in* the scientists, not the scientific method. Far from questioning the right of man to engage in scientific study, the Church has always encouraged it. But the members of Christ's Mystical Body, both clerical and lay, have stood firm in rejecting the tendency of some scientists to go *beyond* the limits of their field.

The rise of modern science was associated very frequently with men who openly rejected all notions of God, of the soul, of the supernatural. Undoubtedly this is why the Catholic Church has so often been accused of opposing science. By some overturning of logic, the rejection of these religious notions was usually associated with the scientific discoveries that these men had made. Any other man who continued to believe in God and things of the spirit seemed "unscientific" as a result. With the passing of time, all of this has become more apparent, and there is undoubtedly less friction between science and religion than formerly. But there is a very delicate question that affects the entire problem, a question that will remain with us always. It is the question of just how much influence a man's religion should possess in regard to his scientific knowledge.

Any proper answer to this question must carefully avoid confusing religion and science. Religion must always remain religion, and science remain science. It must not mean, either, that the Christian scientist will have nothing to offer to the spirit of investigation, as though he were held back by his faith. He must enjoy the same freedom sought by others in his field, and no less than they, he must strive to be as excellent a scientist as possible. His method throughout must be the scientific method; this he must never abandon.

From time to time, however, his faith will enter the picture as a guide in his search for truth. This is especially the case when we are faced with what we know today: a supernatural religion with revealed truth. In this instance, God has gone ahead of the human mind — farther than the mind of man could *ever* go alone — and has called back to us what He sees. What He tells us, however, is no less true than what we see ourselves; quite the reverse: we are *all the more sure* of those truths, because they bear the stamp of His authority. If, at times, it seems to our own clouded vision that things are different from what God says, we are far wiser to trust His words than to change them to match our view.

It is this that presents a problem for the unbelieving scientist. He feels that his freedom has been shackled. He himself, lacking the insight of faith, sees his scientific method as the *sole* source of knowing the truth. The man of faith, on the other hand, recognizes *two* different, but *equally valid,* ways of reaching the truth: the investigations of man and the revelation of God. It is this added knowledge, therefore, that gives the members of Christ something special to contribute to the field of science. They must keep before their fellow scientists the one grave danger of their work: the danger of concluding more than they have proved; the danger of leaping beyond their field.

If a man were able to limit his work to the field of science and never touch upon anything else, he would never face this danger. The chemist or bacteriologist is dealing with the material things of the physical world; these things remain constant. It is only in the *interpretation* of his data that the man of science might fall into error. But he has a difficult time refraining from such interpretation. He feels that he must tell what his findings *mean*. It is natural for man to seek to fit his discoveries into a broader frame, and give a more general interpretation to his conclusions for the benefit of his fellow men. The man who is "pure scientist" and nothing more is hard to find. We naturally think in terms of final and ultimate goals. If a man would so interpret his findings, however, he must tread warily. Many scientists have failed to do that. They had not limited themselves to purely scientific conclusions; they have become philosophers, and have even developed new schools of philosophy.

There is no reason, of course, why the scientist cannot also be a man of philosophy. But when he speaks as a philosopher, and aims at interpreting life, he must realize that he no longer speaks as a scientist at that particular moment. If a man's scientific studies indicate that there was some process of evolution in the physical world, and he concludes that "creation" is a myth, he has gone beyond his field. Or when he formulates the laws of nature, he says more than he has proved if he contends that miracles are impossible. A miracle presupposes these general laws of nature; it is only when they are temporarily suspended that we can even begin to talk of a miracle at all. The *fact* of a miracle can best be shown by the help of science. To prove or disprove the *possibility* of a miracle, however, is the work not of the scientist, but of the philosopher.

Modern science has often touched upon the truths of other fields. Certain men have said that since they could find no soul in their laboratories, man has no soul. Other men have dissected the human body with the utmost of scientific care, and found nothing they might label a "free will" or a "mind." They have, therefore, felt compelled to explain the thought of man by the reactions of his nervous system, and his freedom by chemical changes in his body. And because God cannot be weighed and measured, they have concluded there is no God; He is at most an "unscientific" superstition. But God and the soul, as well as man's mind and free will, are all supposed to be *nonmaterial, nonphysical* things, according to the philosopher.

If they do exist, their existence is proved by fields *other than* physical science; but if there is no God, or we have no soul, *no branch* of physical science can *disprove* them either. These are questions that belong to another field of human knowledge entirely.

In the last analysis, we must seek a blending of all truth in human life, whether we receive it from religion, from philosophy, or from science. The vocation of the Christian scientist is to aid in that blending by warding off false and unjustified conclusions, and by pointing out correct ones. Since men of science will seek to fit their scientific knowledge into some more general framework, he must see to it that the background they choose is the true one. If the scientist is ever to succeed in integrating his findings with the rest of human life, he will need these other truths of faith and reason to guide him; otherwise his interpretation of life will be false and incomplete. The world in which we live is a *supernaturalized* world. It is not a question of having a world of science and reason on the one hand, and a world of faith on the other. There is only *one* world in which we live; science and religion both treat of it. The world of the supernatural is entwined with the natural at every step; the order that results from the union of the two is the only one we know, and the only one under which men live.

Christ must live, then, in the field of science by living in His members whose lifework it is. They cannot abandon the field of science to others, lest these other men should lead the world to false conclusions. If these members of Christ should enter into their scientific work as though there is no God, no revealed truth, they will fail to place their findings in the proper background. Christ will not live among the test tubes and microscopes; He will exercise no influence in that part of life at all. If those members of Christ who choose the life of science keep their faith to themselves, they will harm even the work of science by their neglect.

The role of the Christian engaged in the work of science must, finally, include especially the proposing of high ideals. The most noble element of the scientific vocation lies in its search for truth. The pursuit of the true is something particularly close to the heart of the Christian. Being a member of Him who is "the way, and the truth, and the life," it could not be otherwise. It is the glory of Christ's mystical members to put everything at the service of their divine Head, "to re-establish all things in Christ." The Christian, for that reason, has all the more obligation to be a zealous and an exacting scientist. He, more than all others, should be inflamed with the desire of truth. He is another Christ, and Christ is truth. His purely scientific spirit and skill must be second to none. The spirit of Christ, the spirit of truth, must live in him at all times. And by putting his mind and talent and scientific knowledge in the service of God, he need not fear that he degrades himself. He only ennobles his labor by directing it toward the ultimate source of all knowledge and truth among men. The progress of human knowledge means always a step forward in the service of Christ, for truth itself simply cannot lead away from Him.

CHAPTER XX

THE DIVINE PHYSICIAN

And they brought to him all the sick
. . . and he cured them. . . .

SOME of the most beautiful scenes in the life of our Lord are those which portray His tender regard for the sick and the suffering. The heart of Christ went out to those in need, and in the work of saving men's souls, He showed no lack of concern for their bodies. Surely Christ worked many of His miracles to prove His divinity; such apologetic miracles were necessary. Yet even there, His love for the sick was evident, for He chose to help them even when proving His divine mission.

It is most natural, then, that the members of Christ's Mystical Body should also continue to show a loving concern for the sick. And history shows clearly that this is true. From the very earliest days of Christianity, the Church has been associated with this work of charity, for it is the work of Christ. The large communities of nursing Brothers and Sisters that have arisen throughout the centuries give eloquent testimony to this fact; their principal concern in life is to bring the spirit and the love of Christ to those in bodily pain. The magnificent hospitals developed under the auspices of the Church are obvious proof of this Christian love. They are not merely scientific workshops; they are homes of love. The hands which busy themselves with the many tasks of hospital work are, in reality, the hands of Christ. It is He who keeps watch through the long night and bathes the fevered brow. It is He who bends long hours over the surgical table; He who labors daily in the laboratory, in the X-ray room. Through these mystical members of His, Christ continues to shower His love upon suffering humanity. Through them, He continues to restore health to the weak, sight to the blind, and strength to the lame.

In this way, the many Catholic doctors and nurses and aides throughout the world are really called upon to do the work of Christ. They are not simply doctors or dentists or nurses who happen to be Catholics, nor Catholics who happen to be engaged in the work of medicine. They are, and must be, *Catholic doctors and dentists and nurses.* They must be other Christs in the medical world. They have a share in the apostolate of Christ; they have a mission to fulfill, a mission that no one else can accomplish should they refuse. They are *Christ,* living on in the medical field, caring for the sick; and it is their task to bring to that field the spirit and the ideals of the divine Physician.

The progress of medicine in our modern age has kept pace with the advance of science. For that very reason, however, the practice of medicine has tended to share the spirit of modern science as well — a spirit of irreligion. Large numbers of men have felt that there is something incompatible here. God and miracles and prayer were relegated to the land of medieval superstition. Man was now sufficient to cure his own ills; he had no need to pray to God.

It is a curious situation that the development of man's God-given talents can lead some men away from God and draw others closer to Him. When we view the advances of the medical field in recent years, we might react in either of two ways. It might indicate to us the omnipotence of man, limited only by time and experience in what he might accomplish. Or it might indicate to us the omnipotence of God in giving to mere men the wisdom and the talent to make such progress. In a way, the breath-taking operations performed in our hospitals today are really tributes to God; we might almost be tempted to call them miracles. Fifty years ago, even ten years ago, men would have said that such surgery was absolutely impossible. "What hast thou that thou hast not received?" asked St. Paul of the Corinthians. "And if thou hast received it, why dost thou boast as if thou hadst not received it?" His words have application here. All the talent, all the medical knowledge and skill that a man possesses, come ultimately from God, His Creator. It is all a question of how we look at things. A man may see there his own personal wisdom and skill; or he may see the wisdom of God reflected in him, shared with his poor humanity.

Men and women in the field of medicine have need of that humility in the sight of God no less than others. They need it to help lead men to God, rather than away from Him. And they need it for themselves in time of failure; they need it at those times when they must turn the matter over to God, knowing that He has placed limits upon what man can do, despite his progress. The members of Christ who labor in the field of medicine are best fitted to inject that spirit into their particular little "world." That is one of their tasks. Religion and prayer are vital demands of human life; man reaches out for them as naturally as he desires food and drink. "As the deer longs for the streams of water, so does my soul long for thee, O God." This is especially true in time of suffering and sickness. The heart and the soul of man are not something completely distinct from his body; they are all intimately linked in that oneness that forms the individual. If we try to cure his body without putting his mind and soul at rest, even the bodily cure will be hampered. Faith and medicine can most often work hand in hand for the betterment of those who suffer. The hospital that would exclude God, or the physician who would ignore Him, both run the risk of treating *bodies* well while treating sick *men* and *women* badly.

The failure to fill one's work with the Christian spirit produces an unfortunate result in the treatment of the sick. It means, so often, that we substitute scientific technique for Christian love. The result is the cold, impersonal type of medical care that disregards the individual. It brings about those hospitals where the patient feels like a specimen, forever exposed beneath the lens of a giant microscope. It means an endless round of pills and injections, administered like shots given to so many guinea pigs. It produces the type of doctor who marches down the corridor, solemnly escorted by a band of assistant doctors and nurses and secretaries; the man who asks everything but a pair of trumpets to announce his approach, and who breezes in and out of the rooms like a general inspecting his troops. It is the danger of forgetting that *people* — real human beings — go along with the bodies whose ailments we would cure.

In a way, this shift in spirit merely reflects a general tendency of our age: the tendency to secularize life, to separate it from God and religion. Yet, strange as it seems, if a man boasts that he is devoted only to his fellow men, and has no concern for God, he will eventually harm mankind rather than help. Whenever we put God into the background, we come eventually to think less of man. Instead of becoming more devoted *humanists,* we become less so whenever we concentrate on man to the exclusion of God. The meaning of man and of human life is so intimately bound up with his relationship to God that we cannot slight the one without injuring our notion of the other. Without God we have a false notion of what man is. Indeed, as Cardinal Suhard has pointed out, it is the Christian alone who "will be completely humanist, for (he) alone will be able to offer the civilization in formation a valid norm, a just conception of man." Thus again, the Christian must bring to the field of medicine the total view of human life. If he neglects his apostolate in that area, other gods will spring up. We humans are hopelessly religious. If we refuse to submit to God, we go on to subject ourselves to "science" or "progress" or "the State." Man then becomes something very unimportant in himself; he loses his worth as an individual, and becomes but a tiny, meaningless fragment of the whole picture.

It is only when we have reduced man to this level that we can deal with him on an assembly-line basis; only then can we treat his illness with the same cold, big-business methods by which we put spark plugs into automobile motors. The Christian stands to defend man against this degradation. "It is the Christian idea of human nature, and it alone," wrote Cardinal Suhard, "which will prevent the de-humanization of man." The *real* man is a man dependent upon

God; a man wounded by sin and in dire need of the redeeming grace of Christ. This view alone sees man as he actually is.

The presence of Christ is needed also to ward off a second danger of a science without God. It is the danger of losing all moral principles. The tendency to secularize life also means the tendency to separate morality from other spheres of life. In the field of medicine, it means the cry for "unlimited freedom" in medical practice. Here, as elsewhere, the members of Christ must hold aloft the standards of God. The universal law of right and wrong as pronounced by Christ must be observed in all we do. Without such principles as guides, the men engaged in the field of medicine may well lose their way, and even seek to do an injustice to their fellow men. The sad words of Pius XII were prompted by those men who actually had done so. "To our profound grief we see at times the deformed, the insane, and those suffering from hereditary disease deprived of their lives, as though they were a useless burden to Society; and this procedure is hailed by some as a manifestation of human progress, and as something entirely in accordance with the common good." Religious principles cannot be separated from the practice of medicine, any more than they can be detached from any human activity.

To some men, this sounds as though the Church would interfere in a field not her own. They complain that "the Catholic doctor is in perpetual subordination to the priest in many matters of life and death"; they rant about the "priestly code for the practice of medicine." Actually, the moral code is no more the work of priests than it is the work of physicians or firemen or butchers. The moral law is the work of God, inscribed on the very heart of man. The application of that moral law to particular circumstances is often a difficult task; emotional thinking can frequently stand in the way. But the thought of some secret society of Roman cardinals suddenly whipping up a medical code in the silence of the night, and arbitrarily binding the Catholic world to that code, strikes the Catholic as something highly imaginary. Any set of medico-ethical principles must always be the result of long study and protracted discussion, in which both medical men and moralists play their role.

A medical man needs high principles, but he also needs definite direction for particular situations. A man may use his knowledge to promote artificial birth control, or to effect sterilization, or to procure abortions; it is his set of moral principles that will determine whether he does or not. But when he is faced with a situation in which there is a question, here and now, as to whether what he would do is right or wrong, he needs an immediate answer. If the surgeon sees that he must remove a cancerous growth, and realizes that the procedure will render the man or woman sterile for life, he must understand the moral principles that guide his action. He must be able to see the difference between this case and the removal of a healthy organ merely to effect sterility. A medical code does no more than this. It seeks to form his conscience by meeting these possibilities before they arise in the operating room. And the members of Christ must defend these principles. If they do not, the moral code of expediency will be adopted in its place. We might call it an immoral code, since it would be formulated without reference to any objective religious standard at all. There is, however, no neutral ground. A man must do something in practice, and what he does will necessarily follow some set of moral standards.

Those men and women in the field of medicine must then reflect the spirit of Christ. The moral code means simply acting as Christ Himself would act in the same situation. They are Christ, united to Him in His Mystical Body; they must act for Him and in Him. And as Christ would not be unconcerned with the moral principles of those about Him, neither can those Catholics engaged in this work. As it happens, most of these principles depend upon the natural law, so that there is nothing specifically "Christian" about them; they need not, on that account, be labeled "Catholic" standards. But they do reflect the mind of Christ, so that it becomes the special task of His members to give them to the world.

In everything we do in caring for the sick, whether at home or at a hospital, the Christian must strive to be conscious of his inner oneness with Christ. He must see Christ in himself and in those to whom he ministers. It is the individual that is important, and we must not be concerned with "sickness" as much as we are with "sick people." In healing the sick, as in dying upon the cross, our Lord saw the individual man or woman. He did not die for some vague, unnamed mass of humanity. He died for "you" and for "me." That same spark of personal love should especially be present when, through His members, He reaches out to comfort and cure the sick, and to ease their pain. Christ would not act in a cold, indifferent manner, and His members may not do so either. The Christian has something very special to bring to the medical field. He brings Christian love; He brings the love of Christ.

As Pius XII has pointed out, speaking to a group of nurses: "To recognize Jesus in the invalid and to act yourself like Jesus with him — here is the ideal of every Christian nurse!" The same is true of every individual who deals with the sick. "In this way, it will come about that the image of Christ will be reproduced twice by every bed of pain: in the sick person, the Christ of Calvary expiating and resigned; and in the one assisting, the compassionate Christ, divine doctor of soul and of body."

CHAPTER XXI

THE SUFFERINGS OF CHRIST

O foolish ones and slow of heart . . .
Did not the Christ have to suffer these things
before entering into his glory? . . .

IT MIGHT strike some men as peculiar that, down through the centuries, the followers of Christ have repeatedly chosen the cross as the symbol of their way of life. There were so many events in the life of our Lord that present a happier picture, scenes of joy, of triumph, of victory. Yet the cross has become the glowing symbol of all that Christ and Christianity stand for.

A glance at the life of Christ, however, will show the reason for this choice. Everything in the life of Christ pointed to the cross. It marked the climax of His life upon earth, it was the one event that gave meaning to everything else He did, because it was on Calvary that Christ redeemed mankind. He had scarcely been born when Simeon blessed Him in the temple and said to His Mother: "Behold, this child is destined for the fall and for the rise of many in Israel, and for a sign that shall be contradicted. And thy own soul a sword shall pierce, that the thoughts of many hearts may be revealed."

The entire public life of Christ kept looking toward those three hours on the cross. Our Lord Himself spoke of it with ever increasing clarity as time went on. "Behold, we are going up to Jerusalem, and all things that have been written through the prophets concerning the Son of Man will be accomplished. For he will be delivered to the Gentiles, and will be mocked and scourged and spit upon; and after they have scourged him, they will put him to death; and on the third day he will rise again."

Shortly before He closed His public life, Christ spoke His last words to the people. "The hour has come for the Son of Man to be glorified. Amen, amen, I say to you, unless the grain of wheat fall into the ground and die, it remains alone. But if it die, it brings forth much fruit. . . . Now my soul is troubled. And what shall I say? Father, save me from this hour! No, *this is why I came to this hour*. Father, glorify thy name!" The very same words that Christ spoke in the upper room on that Thursday night before He died: "Father, the hour has come! Glorify thy Son, that thy Son may glorify thee. . . ."

There is in all of this a mystery that strikes at the very heart of Christianity: the mystery of suffering. Pagan peoples have at times thought that their gods were pleased by human suffering; to appease them, they would even offer human sacrifice. The Christian will have none of this. He cannot see in the sufferings of Christ an attempt to satisfy the demands of a god who delights in the sufferings of man; nor can he imagine that Christ had to suffer so much and so terribly because so much more — the salvation of the entire human race — was at stake. It is rather the fact that *Christ* suffers that he would stress, instead of the *sufferings* of Christ. The important thing is that Christ is God, and whatever He does is of infinite value. We know well that Christ might have chosen *any* single act of His life and offered it as the atoning act. He might have redeemed us by simply kneeling down and reciting a prayer. The recitation of that prayer would have been an act of God, and as such it would have possessed the same value as His death upon the cross. Or Christ might have been only scourged or crowned with thorns. It was the fact that God freely chose the death upon the cross that made it the means of redemption. The real question, then, is *why* did God choose the death of His Son to save mankind.

Once again, it is a study of human nature as we find it today that

will give us our answer. Man lives today in a state of "fallen nature";
his is a nature that has been affected by the sin of his first parents.
The special privileges which freed Adam and Eve from all suffering
before they fell are no longer ours. Cast out of the garden of paradise,
the shortcomings of human nature have free rein; we must all know
sorrow and suffering; we must labor and toil in the sweat of our
brow until death. To achieve whatever goals we set before ourselves,
we must undergo hardship, sorrow, weariness, death. All men know
that. There is no easy way of accomplishing anything really worth
while among men; there is a price attached to every triumph. This
will always remain true since mankind will always remain under the
spell of Adam's fall. Not even the redeeming grace of Christ will
make of man's present life a second garden of paradise.

We cannot escape these burdens then, but we can learn how to
carry them. That is the secret of Christianity. By redeeming us,
our Lord did not intend to remove all trial and sorrow from our
life. As with everything else, however, Christ did intend to *transform*
our sufferings, to ennoble them, to glorify them; He wished to take
hold of them and change them inwardly by infusing into them His
spirit of love.

Christ led the way in this work of transformation by laying hold
of His own sufferings, and clothing them with the glory of triumph
and victory. Men had long been accustomed to measuring the worth
of what they did by the hardships involved. They had grown to see a
sign of love in what one man would endure for the sake of another;
and when they saw that a man would give up not merely his
worldly goods, but his very life for the sake of another, they recognized in that the highest sign of love. "Greater love than this no one
has, that one lay down his life for his friends." When Christ, therefore,
sought one act by which He might redeem us and at the same time
give full expression to His eternal love for us, He chose to "lay down
his life for his friends." He never wanted any man to say that Christ
loved him less than someone else who had died in his behalf; Christ
freely chose to suffer and die upon the cross in order to give supreme
proof of His love — a love that knows no equal.

In doing this, Christ also set a pattern for His followers. From

Christ's own example they were to learn how they might take their own sufferings and sorrows, and transform them into means of grace and symbols of victory. He showed us how we might take the suffering of human life that we cannot escape altogether, and lay it upon the altar as a pledge of our love. He showed us how we might take those trials and use them to bring God's blessing down upon men, just as He Himself made use of His sufferings on the cross to restore us to grace.

Redemption may be viewed from two sides: the side of Christ and the side of man. By his death Christ made it *possible* for every man to be saved. He alone did this. "Neither is there salvation in any other. For there is no other name under heaven given to men by which we must be saved." Yet salvation is not an automatic thing, by which Christ saves men without asking anything on their part. True, everything we do in the way of salvation we do under Christ; we do it only because He gives us the power to do it. But under Him, nevertheless, we must *do* something, freely, devotedly, lovingly. Everything that Christ did to save us, He did as an example for us to imitate. Christ prayed, and we must pray; Christ labored for the kingdom of God, and so must we labor also. But Christ also suffered, and so must we.

If ever a man says that he cannot understand suffering in a Christian's life, what he really means is that he has failed to understand suffering in the life of Christ. If only we admit that Christ accomplished His greatest work upon the cross, we can see the value of suffering in our own lives. The Church to which we belong is that same Church "which Christ purchased with His own Blood, and whose members glory in a thorn-crowned Head. The fact that they thus glory is a striking proof," writes Pius XII, "that the greatest joy and exaltation are born only of suffering, and hence that we should rejoice if we partake of the sufferings of Christ, that when His glory shall be revealed we may also be glad with exceeding joy."

It is this that gives meaning even to those lives which appear so wasted to the man without the gift of faith. How many times people will stand over the bed of a young man or woman, doomed to death by some incurable disease, and shake their heads in despair. "He could have accomplished so much; and look now: there is nothing." From the standpoint of Christ, however, this person may accomplish far more by carrying his cross than by anything he had already done or might possibly do in the future. Christ did His greatest work upon the cross; can we not do the same? How can we dare to say that the life of a paralytic, lingering on year after year, is a wasted life? He may accomplish far more than all the healthy men and women about him.

In the life of Christ's Church there will always be, as there was in the life of the God-Man, a cross that must be borne. God asks a certain amount of prayer from each of us, a certain amount of suffering. We may be crushed by our sorrows, and collapse under our cross; or we may raise our eyes to heaven after the manner of Christ, and turn them into triumph. It is this transformation that has made the cross of Christ the symbol of Christianity. It is a process of transformation that must go on daily in our own lives. A toothache, a headache; endless days of mental anguish; long weeks or years upon a bed of pain; the suffering of a hot, sweaty factory; the torture of war; the pangs of childbirth; the terror of death. All of these, and a hundred more, can be transformed under the shadow of the cross. They too can become the means of drawing down God's grace upon us, if only we accept them in the spirit of Christ: "Father, not my will but thine be done."

A man need not feel that sickness holds him back from being of help to those whom he loves; that suffering hinders his labor. Our oneness in Christ has an answer to that difficulty also. Christ suffered not for His own benefit, but for ours. In the same way, although we must each suffer to atone for our own shortcomings, we may also offer our sufferings for the benefit of others. This is what St. Paul meant when he wrote from prison in Rome: "I rejoice now in the sufferings I bear for your sake; and what is lacking of the sufferings of Christ I fill up in my flesh for his body, which is the Church." "For your sake," he writes; "for my fellow members in the Mystical Body of Christ our Lord." Christianity emphasizes the *social* element in everything in life, even in suffering. We are never alone in Christ; for "we though many, are one body." We can help our brethren by doing no more than patiently accepting the sufferings of our daily life and offering them up for others. An eloquent preacher may convert a hardened sinner, but a man confined to a bed of pain may meet with greater success. A great lay apostle may seem to be converting the world when it is really from a little room in a hospital that his success comes. The apostolate of suffering is not an idle apostolate, and certainly not a useless one.

There are, of course, no sufferings lacking in the sufferings of the God-Man. What St. Paul meant was that a certain amount of suffering is expected of every Christian, following the pattern set by Christ. Some men, however, will do no penance; their sins far outweigh their atonement. They rebel at the crosses sent to them by God, and they undergo them because they have no choice; they never accept them. They are, however, members of the Mystical Christ, no less than we. It was for them that Paul suffered, and for whom he would have us suffer also. The Mystical Christ is formed by the God-Man, united to His Mystical Body, the Church. We would make up, then, for what is lacking to the sufferings of this Whole Christ *on the part of His Body,* the Church. In this way, the growth of Christ's Body upon earth will be promoted and the grace of redemption, won upon the cross, will find its rightful place in the hearts of men.

The pagan can see none of this. To him suffering is an insoluble puzzle, sickness a meaningless frustration, and death is despair. But to the man who has "put on Christ," all these things have the meaning of Christ. They become, like us, wrapped up in the redemptive work of our Lord. Trials and sorrows become, in a way, the symbol of a Christian's life, as the cross is a symbol of Christ's. A Christianity that would know no sorrow would have strayed from the path of Christ. "In the world you will have affliction. But take courage, I have overcome the world."

For this reason, the Christian also undertakes various forms of mortification and penance. They have *no* value *apart* from Christ, as though a man could save himself by abstaining from the use of meat one day each week. But done *under Christ,* and through His grace, they possess a value that comes from Christ and His cross. They become, in that way, a means of personal sanctification as well as a means of promoting the spiritual good of our neighbor. Christ lives in us, in all we do; it is Christ who gives a worth to our voluntary mortification.

Suffering and sorrow are thus linked with joy and triumph in the life of Christ's members. It does not mean, of course, that science should cease trying to alleviate the burdens of human life, nor that the field of medicine should give up its attempt to overcome sickness and disease. What it does mean, however, is that even with our very best of attempts, we shall not overcome suffering completely. It will remain in one form or another. The Christian would merely tell the world how to make use of these crosses, knowing, as St. Paul writes, that "as the sufferings of Christ abound in us, so also through Christ does our comfort abound . . . for [we] have been given the favor on Christ's behalf — not only to believe in him but also to suffer for him. . . ."

CHAPTER XXII

THE JUSTICE OF CHRIST

May he rule thy people with justice,
and thy poor with equity. . . .
He shall protect the lowly among the people. . . .

HERE in America, we divide our government into three branches: the executive, the legislative, and the judicial. It is the task of the men in this third branch to enforce the laws of the country. We think first of all, quite naturally, of our judges. They must set the pace. But along with them, there are thousands of others who must also work in the interests of justice: policemen, sheriffs, district attornies, F.B.I. men; special investigators and detectives; prison officials and probation officers. All of these are called upon to dedicate their lives in the interests of the common good. They seek to promote the reign of justice among men. Side by side with them, we must also align the entire legal profession. We might be tempted to think of a lawyer as opposing these official custodians of common justice, as though he must work against them; an unfortunate number of unscrupulous lawyers would certainly give that impression. But the lawyer, no less than the judge or the policeman, is dedicated to the interests of justice. Without that sense of dedication, he will be nothing more than a hypocritical legalist.

Even without Christianity, there would undoubtedly have been such law-enforcing agencies in human society. As life grew more

complex, men would have seen the need of assigning to certain ones
the protection of life and property, both in the name of the community and the individual. But just as Christianity reaches down and
envelops everything in human life, so also does it ennoble these tasks.
There is a justice that is proper to Christ, and a charity flowing from
Him that tempers justice. And it is this justice and this charity that
the members of Christ must bring to these professions. There is an
honor and an integrity that is a part of justice, and the members of
Christ must exert themselves to promote that honor in their field
of work.

Perhaps it is a rather harsh view to think of Christ living in
those who deal with the law; we are accustomed to think of our
Lord only in terms of meekness and patience. Yet He Himself has
told us that He has a concern for justice, and it is this same Lord
of Love who will return at the end of the world as an Exacting Judge.
To the evil He will say: "Depart from me, accursed ones, into the
everlasting fire which was prepared for the devil and his angels."
But to the good: "Come, blessed of my Father, take possession of
the kingdom prepared for you from the foundation of the world."
In a way, the search for justice and the punishment of crime in
human society is a figure of that final day. It is something bound up
entirely with the success or the failure of a Christian way of life.
We can never promote justice and root out crime and refashion criminals without Christianity. That is why Christ must live in His members engaged in this work. They have the solution, the *only* solution;
they must bring that solution to light; they must make His presence
felt in these circles.

When we understand the Christian teaching about original sin, we
are not too amazed to find that there is vice and crime among men,
that they lie and cheat and rob. Human nature was not completely
corrupted by the fault of Adam, but it was weakened. Without the
grace of God, man cannot even keep the requirements of the natural
law — the Ten Commandments — for any length of time. If men
neglect the grace of God, and the means of obtaining it, they will
break these commandments; and because of our social nature, it is
inevitable that sooner or later such disregard for virtue will bring

some men into conflict with the rest of society. This conflict may arise on the civil level, with all its complicated problems of ownership and possession, wills and debts, patents and legal rights. The laws of the country must be upheld on all these points; justice must prevail. Or the conflict may also arise on the level of crime; it then becomes the duty of the law-enforcing agencies to protect society from those at fault.

None of this, however, can be accomplished without the aid of Christianity. Justice will not prevail nor crime cease until men have learned to derive their moral strength from the only source at hand: until they have learned to live by the strength of Christ. Christ must live in society, but especially on these vital levels. He must walk the beat with every policeman; He must sit at the side of every judge. He must live in the prison warden, the detectives, the federal investigators, the lawyers. Through them, the reign of Christ's justice will be brought about on this earth. A man cannot be a Christian one day and a "neutral" the next. He cannot put his faith off into a little corner of his life, far removed from his daily activity. The spirit of Christ must fill every nook and cranny of his life. If it does not, his life can know only failure. To ignore the Christian way of life is to deny it; there is no middle path. Traditionally, our courts have drawn their strength from a belief in God. If that is cast aside, to what purpose will we administer oaths in our courtrooms? As our Supreme Court declared in 1892: "This (the United States) is a religious people. This is historically true. From the discovery of this continent to the present hour, there is a single voice making this affirmation." And "this official conjunction of the laws of God with the Constitutions and laws of the land is," as Clarence Manion comments, "the basic and controlling ingredient of Americanism."

It goes without saying, then, that those men who would mirror Christ on this level must be most exacting in their own justice. As the prophet said of Christ, they must "protect the lowly among the people," and "save the children of the poor" and "crush the oppressor." A lawyer may never be satisfied with merely "handling a case." Certainly the interests of the oppressed are not provided for by a lawyer who is careless and slipshod; nor is society benefited by a legalist who trims the facts of the case to serve his purpose, and who, like the Pharisees of old, attempts to twist the meaning of the law according to his own desires. Family life is not strengthened by lawyers who look upon "divorce" as a good synonym for "a fee."

A policeman who connives at crime, who takes his "cut" in return for silence does not have the mind of Christ. His faith must walk the beat with him; it is not something for Sunday Mass alone. An investigator who overlooks abuses as a "favor" to a friend, is betraying the trust placed in him by his fellow men. A district attorney or a detective who would present false evidence or lie in court merely to ensnare a criminal, however bad he may be, is not serving the interests of justice. There is a need for a wholesome idealism in all this work, a Christian idealism. Honesty and integrity are the watchword; Christ would settle for nothing less.

The judge especially needs the spirit of Christ in all he does; if the courts become corrupt, our last hope is gone. The integrity of our legal system depends above all upon the integrity of those who administer it, and it is Christianity that insures this integrity and raises it to the level of the divine. Court procedure itself has shown this influence of religion in asking the witness to swear upon the Word of God to speak the truth. If religion be abandoned, the foundations of our system of law will be lost. Our court trials will become nothing more than a meaningless battle of words, with victory awarded to cleverness rather than to truth.

Christianity has something further to bring to this field. The spirit of Christ is the spirit of love. As for the criminal, the pagan spirit was the spirit of revenge; the men of the Old Testament sought "an eye for an eye and a tooth for a tooth." But Christ brought a new law. "I say to you, love your enemies, do good to those who hate you, and pray for those who persecute and calumniate you. . . ." If a man is a criminal, it is not enough for society to "get even" with him. Christian love would reach out and attempt to help the criminal find himself; it would seek to refashion the man, and redirect the youth. This is not to imply that society has no right to protect itself from those who have stifled the voice of social conscience. It surely has. The world of criminals is carefully circumscribed within the limits of their own personal interest. Sometimes they must even be protected from themselves.

But despite that, society is not absolved from all obligation in this regard especially not a Christian society. As time goes on, we are turning more and more attention to the fact that it is far more sensible to prevent things than correct them after they have taken place. Periodic medical examinations are advised for those who don't even feel sick; great interest has been developed in accident and fire prevention. But crime prevention seems to have gotten off to a slower start. It deals far more directly with human beings and would seem even more important than these others. But the human element makes the problem just that much more complex; perhaps that is one of the reasons for the apathy. But it is a sad commentary that authorities should still speak of our treatment of men in prison as the "last great shame left in America," claiming that most Americans are supposed to be more aware of Russian slave labor camps than of injustices in their local police lockups. Here is a task for the Christian. Any plan of crime prevention that eliminates or ignores God and religious values is doomed to failure. No matter how "modern" and "progressive" a theory it may represent, without the grace of Christ it cannot know success.

It is the special task of the followers of Christ to temper justice with the love of Christ. A reform school ought really to try to reform, and not just punish, a youth. A prison term should mean an opportunity at readjustment instead of a postgraduate course in crime. The most common source of crime is found to be a lack of love; psychologists call it a failure to feel "accepted." Usually, somewhere in the background we will find some sort of rejection by one or many that has made the individual feel he does not "belong." He takes it out on society. As a defense for his own feelings, he builds a wall about himself, and encases himself within; he becomes calloused, and stifles his conscience as much as he can, so that he can more easily walk upon others and take advantage of them. As a rule, of course, he does all of this unconsciously. Like others, he himself may see the finished product, but he may be confused about what it really is, and how it got to be what it is. Ideally, it would be far more logical to seek to prevent such antisocial tendencies from ever arising at all; this is the concern of every branch of society: the family, the school, the community. It means implanting in the heart of every child a truly Christian love. Anyone who has tried his hand at it knows how difficult it is to reshape the mind and habits of a hardened criminal or even of a misdirected youth. Yet we can hardly give way to the gloomy theory of Lombroso that some men are simply born criminals and nothing can be done about it. Christian hope rises above such feelings of despair.

Christ would never be indifferent or calloused to such a situation; the Christian may not be either. Granted that the task is a thankless one, often, and an exasperating one, there is all the more need of Christian love to inspire it, and Christian patience to endure it. Anyone can see the danger to society of maladjusted criminals, but the Christian can gaze with the eyes of Christ and see far more. He can see the bitterness and frustration, the overwhelming burden of unhappiness and despair that lurks beneath that outer shell of harshness and antagonism. He can pierce through the outward appearances, and see the utter ruin and failure of those lives, the bitter sorrow that pursues them at every step. He can also see the role that society itself has had in bringing about this failure. We cannot hope to produce a country of men filled with the ideals of justice, if we insist on calling big-time racketeers nothing more than "clever businessmen." We cannot root out crime on a small scale when we defend and even idealize it on a large scale. We cannot draw "little men" to the love of virtue, when the first-rate corruption of a sheriff or a district attorney or even a judge is the topic of daily gossip on the street corner.

Honor and justice and equity; charity and patience: these are the virtues of Christ that the Christian can bring to this work. The spirit of Christ must help to correct what has been done, and to avoid a recurrence of the same situation in the lives of these and others. This means aiming our efforts at the family, the school, the social community. These must be made truly Christian if we are to promote justice, avoid crime, and fill society with the Christian spirit. *They* must succeed, if the work of the lawyer, the judge, the law-enforcing agencies is ever to succeed. No man does his job alone, especially in this difficult matter. It is, assuredly, an overwhelming task, but it is ultimately the only solution: the solution of Christ. Otherwise we shall be doing no more than trying, halfheartedly, to fill the holes in a leaky dike.

CHAPTER XXIII

RELIGIOUS LIFE

If thou wilt be perfect,
go sell what thou hast,
and give to the poor,
. . . and come, follow me. . . .

EVERY member of the Church of Christ must do what he can to make his own life more Christlike. Bishops and priests, of course, are called upon to continue the very work of Christ in preaching, in offering the Sacrifice of the Mass, and in administering the Sacraments. Their *official* oneness with Christ, stemming from their ordination, demands that they strive to make their own lives shining examples of holiness. The members of the laity, in turn, must work to Christianize their daily activities. Their families, their work, their recreation; their political life, their economic life, their educational life — all must mirror, in some way, the spirit of Christ. In all they do they must "have this mind . . . which was also in Christ Jesus." In that way alone will the presence of Christ be felt throughout the vast encompass of this world that He would make His own.

Apart from these two groups, however, there is a third group of great importance. It marks a special vocation in the Church, the vocation to the *religious life*. It is formed by those men and women who join together under their own superiors in order to live a more Christian way of life. Whereas the laity must strive to make their daily lives more Christian, the religious adopt as their *principal* goal in life the imitation of Christ. Their primary concern is to become more Christlike. Whatever work they might undertake within the limits of their vocation, it may never replace this primary task which they have freely assumed. They are the men and women who would accept the words of Christ at face value, and attempt to put them into practice in a most strict fashion. They accept not only the commands of Christ, but His counsels. "If thou wilt enter into life, keep the commandments," said Christ to the rich young man. "All these I have kept," he answered, "ever since I was a child." And our Lord said to him in turn: "One thing is still lacking to thee; sell all that thou hast, and give to the poor, and thou shalt have treasure in heaven; and come, follow me."

A man or a woman becomes a religious in order to give greater glory to God and His Church upon earth, and to secure his or her own perfection by practicing the evangelical counsels. Christ did not order all His members to undertake this life, although He wishes its *spirit* to dwell in each member. He did exhort His followers, however, to do more, if they would; He encouraged them not only to live in the spirit of poverty and chastity and obedience, but to embrace these practices as the rule of their life. For that reason, the religious life as it has developed in the Mystical Body marks a high point in man's imitation of Christ our Head. It sets a pattern for the rest of the Body. The religious promises publicly to strive with all his might to model his life as closely as possible upon the life of the God-Man; he does so in order that, like St. Paul, he might say to the others in all humility: "Be imitators of me as I am of Christ."

The sight of a brother or a nun, clothed in their unusual robes, is always something of a puzzle to the nonbeliever. Yet, confused though he may be, he cannot but sense something special, something "set apart" about these people. They are continual reminders of an entire world that the unbeliever would ignore. They make it more difficult for him to do so. It is easy enough to ignore the words that someone may speak, but when you see intelligent, mature men and women giving up everything in order to put those words into practice, you find it more difficult to set that other world aside. The religious priest also would speak this same message to the world. As a priest, he would surely have to strive for the same degree of sanctity even if he were not a religious, but now he has a twofold reason for making Christ live in him personally.

The religious life in the Church is marked by four qualities: it involves a fixed or stable manner of life, lived in common; it is a life in which the evangelical counsels are observed, by means of the vows of poverty, chastity, and obedience. It has known a gradual growth in the Church, and each succeeding generation has witnessed the rise of new communities devoted to reproducing some special perfection in the life of Christ. Some emphasize above all His life of prayer; others His life of teaching, of charity, of caring for the sick, or rescuing the sinner. Some limit themselves to a purely contemplative life, spending their entire lives in prayer and penance within the confines of their monastery; others enter into an active life of some sort. Yet all of them embrace this stable common life, strengthened by their threefold vows. Because of these, no matter what work they do, their common and basic purpose must always be to reflect the image of Christ. So also must the members of the Secular Institutes mirror this image. Though remaining in the world, they are bound by their vows to the pursuit of this evangelical perfection. They must all give up whatever worldly attachments might hinder their spiritual progress.

They set aside, first of all, the right to possess anything of the world. Like Christ Himself, who "had nowhere to lay his head," they seek to be completely poor. It is most natural for a man to want *something* that is his own, and yet that very tendency to possess things can drag a man down. He can become so attached to what he owns that his possessions take first place in his life. To eliminate this danger, the religious gives it all up in one act of surrender. From then on he is obligated to poverty.

This is a subtle thing. It is the spirit that matters. Any religious knows what a struggle it is to keep fighting this tendency to possess. Most often the religious is not poor in the sense that he is starving or homeless. Indeed many persons in the world have enforced upon them by circumstance a poverty that far outstrips the poverty of the religious. But this very security seeks to assert itself, and a man may tend to forget that what he uses is not really his own; or he may eventually fail to see that it really makes much difference. A Sister might be horrified, for example, to find that she is as much attached to the habit of her order as she could be to a Cadillac convertible; should a situation arise where the habit might need to be abandoned or changed, she might feel as though someone were tearing her very heart away. But it is precisely because the religious realizes just how deep this tendency does go, that he strives to give up so much. It is not a sin to own something, and a millionaire could really be entirely detached from his possessions. But it would be harder, perhaps, than if he actually gave up such ownership once and for all. The religious strives to make his progress in things spiritual just that much easier by trying to remove any obstacles. The vow of poverty will not automatically make a man poor in spirit, and keep him that way; but it will certainly make it easier.

For the same reason, the religious gives up the joy and happiness of rearing a family. The desires of the flesh are not wrong in themselves, and the vows of religious life do not even hint they are. But, as St. Paul says, "He who is unmarried is concerned about the things of the Lord, how he may please God. Whereas he who is married is concerned about the things of the world, how he may please his wife; and he is divided." Now again, this does not come about automatically. Obviously, an unmarried man can be concerned with a good many worldly things, and not at all about God; but a husband *cannot* be unconcerned about his wife and children. Those very cares might make it more difficult for the religious to serve God with that liberty of spirit he desires; it would surely make it more difficult to continue in his pursuit of complete poverty, because he would be constantly concerned about the needs of those dependent upon him. The religious seeks, like Paul, to be "free from care," that he might imitate Christ more perfectly.

As with the priest when he assumes a vow of celibacy, the religious is giving up the exercise of one of his most treasured gifts: the capacity to love and to be loved in the intimate sanctuary of marriage and family life. He must replace it with a supernatural love, a love of God, and a love of all mankind in God. If he does not, his spirit will wither away. He is not turning his back upon other men, actually; he is turning toward them. The vow of chastity shows not a denial of love but an enlargement of its scope. The man or woman who gives up the personal, intimate love that is natural to man, does so only that he or she may love with a divine love: an endless, eternal, all-embracing love that envelops the whole of mankind.

That is why the religious life has invariably sought to express itself in some act of kindness toward other men. The religious teacher brings to his work not only knowledge and skill, but the love of God; it is this that can make so much difference. The nursing Sister is not merely a trained nurse; she is a woman dedicated by vow to making the image of Christian *love* shine forth in what she does. The religious social worker is not only a well-trained professional; he or she must be a social worker who gives to all the world an outstanding example of how *Christ Himself* would accomplish those tasks. The missionary especially can show us the love of Christ, for he is not simply a man who talks about the truth of Christ; the missionary is a man (or woman) who also enables pagan hearts to *experience* the warmth of Christ's love.

In order to clear the path to perfection as completely as possible, the religious surrenders one last thing. It is something more difficult to give up than those things contained in the vows of poverty and chastity. The vow of obedience means offering up that very power that gives a man his special dignity; it means surrendering his free will. Community life, like any social group, would be unthinkable without a certain amount of such submission. Men simply cannot live in society without delegating certain powers to one or another individual who serves as the leader. But religious obedience goes far beyond that. In striving to imitate his Redeemer, the religious cries out with Him: "I seek not my own will, but the will of him who sent me." He sees in his superiors the authority of God. He places himself at their disposal completely, to be used as they see fit in accomplishing the tasks assigned to the community.

This is no doubt the hardest of all the vows. It takes away so much, and it demands so great a trust in the providence of God. The individual sees only a man or a woman who happens to be superior. Humanly speaking, he may disagree with the decisions of the superior, and yet, in all that is not sin, he must obey, trusting in the power of God. Even should he not disagree, however, no man likes to take orders; the mere fact that he has been *told* to do this or that raises a difficulty. Yet sin is in the will, and it is only through disciplining that faculty that a man can gain control over his own life. That is the purpose of this vow. "If anyone loves the world, the love of the Father is not in him," wrote St. John; "because all that is in the world is the lust of the flesh, and the lust of the eyes, and the pride of life; which is not from the Father, but from the world." Chastity seeks to curb the lust of the flesh, and poverty seeks to set aside a concern for whatever material possessions the eyes may fall upon. But obedience seeks to root out pride, and that means reaching into the very depths of man's soul: for "pride is the beginning of all sin." It is here that man is weakest, and it is at that very point that his sinful nature rebels most frequently and resists control most stubbornly.

That the image of Christ might appear most vividly throughout the world, God has provided for the growth of religious life. But the religious must think not only of giving example to others; he must also take unto himself all of their trials and cares; he must make his own the concerns of the universal Church. His prayer, his work, his whole life must be lived upon this *world-wide* basis. He has given up what he has of his own, only that he might assume the far broader interests and concerns of Christ for all mankind.

Each congregation, of course, has been founded to meet some special need in the history of the Church; each group, therefore, has its own special message, some special word of Christ to speak. Its chief labor may be teaching or nursing or social work; care of the aged, of orphans; missionary work. Its dominant spirit may be the pursuit of truth, the practice of poverty, the submission of obedience; it may be marked by its special devotion to Mary, to the Sacred Heart, the Trinity, the Good Shepherd, the Divine Word, the Holy Spirit, the Passion of our Lord. But whatever its special message, the lesson will reach the world only if the members of these religious congregations live wholeheartedly according to the spirit of their rule. The example of their lives, the spirit which hovers over them, will tell men what words may not. Theirs is a message that must be *lived*. It is for that reason so much more difficult than merely speaking words; but it is also, for that same reason, so much more beautiful, and so much more forceful.

CHAPTER XXIV

CONTEMPLATIVES AND MISSIONARIES

. . . Go into the whole world
and preach the gospel to every creature.
. . . He went out to the mountain to pray
and continued all night in prayer to God.

THERE are many lessons that the members of Christ's Mystical Body can learn from the lives of His religious. Their devoted imitation of Christ sets the pace for many a work in the Church. There must always be adaptation, of course. The laity are not religious, and their spiritual and apostolic life cannot be simply a miniature of the convent or the monastery. But it is the spirit that is of prime importance; this never changes, for it is the spirit of Christ throughout.

There are two groups of religious, however, that puzzle the ordinary man. Of one group he often asks too much; to the other, he frequently fails to give sufficient credit. The first group would be the missionaries, and the second, the contemplatives.

There is little possibility that any Catholic could fail to realize the need for the missionary life. The words of Christ are eminently clear and demanding: "Go into the whole world and preach the gospel to every creature." From the dawn of Christianity until this present hour, men have left their own land and journeyed to distant countries in order to plant the seed of faith in the hearts of their fellow men. It is a task that will continue until the end of time.

The danger for the ordinary member of the Church, though, is that he may forget that this missionary vocation enters into the very essence of the Church. At the very heart of the Mystical Body, we find this demand of preaching the Gospel to all men, at all times, in all places. It is something universal; it lays an obligation upon every single member — the obligation of being mission-minded. No missionary priest or Sister sets out upon his or her journey alone. They are merely the representatives of so many other members of Christ's Body. In these individual missionaries, all the other members find expression for their missionary vocation. They are contained in these individual apostles, represented by them.

The missions, for that reason, must ever be the concern of every single member of the Church. Those who go forth need help; they need prayer, above all, but they also need financial assistance. They should not have to ask for it, however, as though they were hounding others to give something for their own "private" apostolate. They have, quite the contrary, placed themselves at the service of the entire Church. They need only mention that they are leaving, and it should be apparent at once that the other members who cannot leave their homes for foreign lands must offer whatever assistance they can. The missionary vocation is not limited to those who do the actual work. It is the universal vocation of the members of Christ.

The doctrine of the Mystical Body gives special prominence to that truth. The organic oneness that joins the members of Christ extends all around the world. It is not limited to our own family, our own parish or diocese. If there is a struggling community of Catholics in faraway China, they have a call upon our prayers and our help. The Church that is being formed in Africa should have a place in our daily prayers; and the pastor of the impoverished Negro parish in Mississippi should be able to depend upon others throughout the country to help build a church for their brothers in Christ.

Today there is another fact we might forget about the missions, and that is that they are not limited to foreign lands. We repeat the words of Cardinal Suhard in this regard: "In the Middle Ages, and even up to the nineteenth century, Christianity was localized on the planet, and the missionary apostolate was geographical. Missionaries left Christendom to go and preach to heathen nations. Paganism was outside the Christian world. Today, on the contrary, the two Cities are no longer outside each other but one within the other and closely interlaced. Pagan society penetrates everywhere the daily life of Christians. At present, a closed Christian society, cut off from pagan influence, has become, it seems, unthinkable. France is not the only country to have become a 'missionary country.' More evident in France, the phenomenon is latent everywhere and, no doubt, will become more and more obvious."

This means the apostolate. Not only by aiding the foreign missions must the other members of Christ exercise their missionary vocation; *they themselves* must become active within their own environment. The Christian in our modern world cannot be indifferent to this need. "His manner of acting is imposed upon him by the milieu he lives in: it is the action of leaven. Without moving, he finds himself called to the duty and the work of a missionary." There is much work to be done on all sides, and there is no greater blessing that these modern "home" missionaries can receive than a generous supply of that inspired zeal which stands out so strikingly in those who leave for foreign lands. There has been a tendency to "let well enough alone," and a desire not to allow the laity to become too active in the apostolate, lest they might get out of hand. Because of this, Cardinal Suhard concludes, "our Catholic community, which has constantly sent its sons and daughters to distant lands, has too long forgotten or even suspected this missionary action where one is. The result is an attitude of defense which still expresses itself in our times by an extra-ordinary force of inertia." This is not the spirit of Christ, for a missionary accomplishes nothing by doing nothing, or by simply "holding his own" against the onslaught of pagan forces.

The second group of religious from whom the members of Christ can learn much is formed by the contemplatives. It is to this group that we sometimes fail to give sufficient credit. Some of those who misunderstand their lives complain that they are antisocial. "What good are they?" they ask. "They have abandoned society, and have turned their backs on their fellow men; they do no good for anyone else, they are nothing more than self-centered, frustrated neurotics!" No one was ever more wrong in his judgment of any group of people. The true contemplative is exactly the opposite. He is of great value to mankind and the Church; he is not unconcerned with his fellow men, and he is anything but self-centered and neurotic.

If everything that our Lord did upon earth must be continued through the members of His Mystical Body, the same is true of the long nights He spent upon the mountaintops in prayer. The Mystical Christ must also seek out the solitude of the hillsides and the valleys; the Church must also spend the long nights in prayer. If only we admit that those hours of prayer were not wasted hours in the life of Christ, we can see that they are not wasted in the life of His Church. The work of the Mystical Body is entirely supernatural. Any progress that is really achieved, comes as the result of God-given grace. Prayer, then, is one of the chief means of drawing that grace down upon the Church on earth; it is so necessary that this prayer never cease. It is only logical, therefore, that the Church should delegate certain members to devote their entire lives to that office. "Unless the Lord build the house, they labor in vain who build it."

The danger we find in our modern attitudes is that of wanting to do everything on an assembly-line basis. We feel we must do something; we are activists. Certain members of the Church would want to organize it like the General Motors Corporation or United States Steel. We must do big things on a big scale; but at all costs we must do something. Get people organized; have committees, clubs, rallies, campaigns; build more churches and start more newspapers and send out more envelopes. And when, in such an atmosphere, we find men and women who do nothing but lock themselves in a monastery, it is not surprising that some members begin to feel that these monks are laying down on the job. They aren't doing anything!

The progress of the Church can never be measured by building projects and midnight rallies. Its essential task is something far more subtle; it seeks to refashion men's souls according to the image of Christ. This is a work of prayer and grace, and it is in the accomplishment of this fundamental work that the lives of our cloistered religious are most effective. A talented editor may attract a large group of readers and seem to be instrumental in gaining many converts to the Church; but it may be the life and prayers of a cloistered nun, hidden from the world, that have won the graces that brought about those conversions. The doctrine of the Mystical Body enables us to realize this, because, like a human body, we all act as a unit. No man accomplishes anything in the Church alone. "I have planted," wrote St. Paul, "Apollos watered, but God has given the growth."

That is why the Pope of Catholic Action, Pius XI, could speak of the contemplative vocation in such a laudatory fashion. "It was highly important for the Church," he wrote, "that there should never be lacking men of prayer who, unimpeded by any other care, would be perpetually besieging the Divine Mercy and thus draw down from heaven benefits of every sort upon men, too neglectful of their salvation. . . ." And he concludes with this almost shocking statement: "It is easy to understand how those who assiduously fulfill the duty of prayer and penance contribute *much more* to the increase of the Church and the welfare of mankind than those who labor in tilling the Master's field." It is a statement that shocks only those, however, who forget the essentially spiritual work that belongs to the Church. For those who understand the life of the Mystical Body, the seemingly lonely monastery is a *center* of apostolic activity.

Actually, far from becoming antisocial and turning their backs upon the world, the contemplatives do just the opposite. There is undoubtedly no place in the entire world where men live a more completely *social-minded* life than in the cloister; there is no place where the cares and trials of all men are taken to heart more completely, and where the concerns of others are emphasized more consistently. It is here that the Divine Office, the official prayer of the Church, is recited with the greatest solemnity. We see here the pattern of prayer that should fill the entire Church. We find the spirit that should warm the hearts of priests and religious everywhere, who are obliged to recite the Office in the name of the whole Church; we find the spirit, furthermore, that should enter into the prayer of *every* member of Christ's Mystical Body: the spirit of love, of divine unity; the consciousness of the social bonds between us, and a concern for the needs of the entire Body.

Abbot Marmion, the Benedictine, was once asked how he prepared for the recitation of the Office. His response is the answer of one filled with the true Catholic spirit. "Before reciting the Divine Office, after I have made an act of Faith in Christ, present in my heart through grace, I unite myself to Him in giving praise to His Father. I ask Him to pay special tribute to His Blessed Mother, to the saints — especially those of the day — and to my patron saints.

"Then, I unite myself to Christ as the Head of the Church, as the supreme, though invisible, Pontiff, so that I might plead the cause of the entire Church.

"And for that purpose, I pause to think of those throughout the world who are in need and sorrow: the sick, the dying, the tempted, the hopeless, the sinners, the afflicted. I try to place within the bounds of my own heart, all the sorrow, all the anguish, all the hopes of every single soul. I direct my attention to all the works of zeal undertaken by the members of Christ's Church: the lonely missionaries far away, the teachers, the preachers, the workers. . . .

"And I remember especially those who have sought my prayers, and those who have a call upon my prayers, so that I might intercede for them all with Christ, Who is 'ever living, and making intercession for us.'"

To live and to pray in that spirit is the vocation of every member of Christ. The contemplative sets the example. In the solitude of his cell and the quiet of his chapel, he teaches us how to be truly social-minded; he tells us what it really means to be living members of this social body of Jesus Christ, which is the Church. Very often, today, we label as a "neurotic" someone who does something that we ourselves do not do; since we pray so badly, perhaps, we might consider the contemplative unusual; and since we have so little concern for penance, we might look upon his penances as an indication of some psychological quirk. If dedicating one's entire life to the interests of your fellow men is a sign of something unusual, however, the world could use more "neurotics" of that type. A man or a woman who gives over his or her life to drawing down upon mankind the graces of God cannot be accused of being antisocial; those who are doing more than any others for the good of their fellow men cannot be called neurotic; and most of all, those who have learned to live fully the life of Christ cannot be described as frustrated and unhappy. Behind every cross there is a crown, and beneath every tear there is laughter. The contemplative, like the Apostles, has felt the force of Christ's warning: "Amen, amen, I say to you, that you shall weep and lament, but the world shall rejoice; and you shall be sorrowful, but your sorrow shall be turned into joy." In following Christ even up to Gethsemani, and in spending the long nights in prayer, they have known also His concern, His agony for the world. But they know more. They know well that Christ has called them on, and that Christ stands at their side, whispering to each soul that He has come that "my joy may be in you, and that your joy may be made full."

POURED OUT IN SACRIFICE

As for me, I am already
being poured out in sacrifice. . . .

CHRIST lives on among men, ever seeking to refashion a Christian world. What does not begin upon the altar, however, will not succeed. "Unless the grain of wheat fall into the ground and die, it remains alone; but if it die, it brings forth much fruit." The Christian must put aside the standards of this world before he can understand it; he must abandon the world before he can save it; he must lose his life in Christ and die to the world before he can find his life and live. He must make his own the concerns of Christ, the loves of Christ, the mission of Christ. And he must take them all, and himself as well, and lay them upon the altar of Christ to dedicate them, to sanctify them, to Christianize them. It is only through sacrifice that the world shall be redeemed.

"I exhort you therefore, brethren, by the mercy of God, to present your bodies as a sacrifice, living, holy, pleasing to God — your spiritual service. And be not conformed to this world, but be transformed in the newness of your mind. . . ." Christ must first live in the individual if He is to live in the world, and so the individual must take his life to the altar. He must learn to live the Mass in the sense that he dedicates his life there to God, and allows the sanctifying influence of that worship to influence every corner of his life.

" 'At this altar, let innocence be in honor, let pride be sacrificed, anger slain, impurity and every evil desire laid low, let the sacrifice of chastity be offered in place of doves, and instead of the young pigeons, the sacrifice of innocence.' While we stand before the altar, then, it is our duty so to transform our hearts, that whatever sin there is may be completely blotted out, while whatever promotes supernatural life through Christ may be zealously fostered and strengthened, even to the extent that, in union with the immaculate Victim, we become a victim acceptable to the eternal Father."

It is at the altar that the families of the world will derive the strength to follow Christ; it is there that the bishops, the priests, the religious, the workers and doctors and writers and cab drivers of the world will gain the grace of dedicating their lives entirely to Christ; it is at the foot of this Calvary that the sick and the dying will receive the courage to suffer "in Christ," that the needy will look for help, and the sinner for hope. All Christians meet at the foot of the altar, and it is there that they take to heart the trials and cares of these "other Christs," their fellow members in the Mystical Body of the Redeemer.

Christ now lies prostrate on a bed of pain; we cannot be indifferent. He walks the corridors of the Vatican, ruling the Church; He cares for the infant, and teaches the man; He rescues the sinner, and converts the unbeliever; He teaches men how to find laughter without sin, and literature without the dregs of sex. These are all our concerns. Our heart is boundless as the love of Christ.

Halfway across the world, Christ stands upon a hilltop, defending His home; down the street, He protects His business from the racketeers who would ruin Him, or seeks the right to labor with dignity. He stands beneath the lights of the surgeon or sits at the desk of a congressman. Within the wills of His cloister He continually raises His voice in prayer. Outside His mission chapel He stands alone, looking at the sea. He raises His eyes from His workbench; He kneels at the altar of God; He lifts his hand in absolution and anoints the senses of the dying; He teaches children how to pray. On all sides, we must take note. This is Christ. This is the work of Christ. These are our concerns.

Everything in the life of the Mystical Body prepares for the altar, for the priesthood, for sacraments and sacrifice. "When the Church teaches us our Catholic faith, and exhorts us to obey the commandments of Christ, she is paving an open way for her priestly, sanctifying action in its highest sense. . . . Not only through her ministers, but with the help of the faithful individually, who have imbibed in this fashion the spirit of Christ, the Church endeavors to permeate with this same spirit, the life and labors of men — their private and family life, their social, even economic and political, life — that all who are called God's children may reach more readily the end He has proposed for them. . . . The most pressing duty of Christians is to live the liturgical life, and increase and cherish its supernatural spirit. . . . To participate in the Eucharistic sacrifice is their chief duty and supreme dignity."

This is human life. This is the life we must sanctify, that we must rebuild to the image of Christ. "For me, to live is Christ." Human life has no deeper meaning; it has no other meaning whatsoever. What Jesus of Nazareth began in time must never end until eternity; what He would do now, must be done by those who are His members. All of this that we call human life must be lifted up into our arms, and carried to the foot of the cross; all of this must we pour out in sacrifice upon the altar of Christ, that He might ennoble and refashion it.

It is Christ, and Christ alone, who would save mankind, and give glory to the heavenly Father: the *Whole Christ,* the *Mystical Christ.* Christianity can never settle for a mere "churchgoing" people, or a faith that remains locked within the secret heart of man. "I have come to cast fire upon the earth, and what will I but that it be kindled?" Christianity has a world-shaking mission to accomplish, an apostolate to fulfill. It is a total way of life, all-embracing, all-consuming. But it is a mission that begins, now as always, upon Calvary; it proceeds from the altar. The members of Christ's Mystical Body may never rest until all men "have this mind . . . which was also in Christ Jesus." They may know no peace until they see all of mankind gathered about the altar of Christ, and "by Him and with Him and in Him," giving all honor and glory for ever and ever to God the Father Almighty, in the unity of the Holy Ghost. They may not rest until they find all men at this altar, sanctifying their lives in Christ; they will not achieve victory until they hear the voice of every man echo and re-echo across the entire compass of the earth, those startling words of Paul: "It is now no longer I that live, but Christ lives in me!"